ALGIERS TO ANZIO
WITH 72 & 111 SQUADRONS

FIRST EDITION
published in 2002
by
WOODFIELD PUBLISHING
Woodfield House, Babsham Lane, Bognor Regis
West Sussex PO21 5EL, England.

ISBN 1-873203-68-3

Algiers to Anzio

WITH 72 & 111 SQUADRONS

GREGGS FARISH

WITH MICHAEL McCAUL

Woodfield

This book is dedicated to:

Francesca de Ruggiero Farish,
my wife, married July 7th, 1947

Our children:
Anne, Catharine, Joseph, Mary

Our grandchildren:
Sarah, Amelia, Andrea, Stefania, Kieran,
Kelly, Charlotte, Catharine and Greggs

Contents

Greggs Farish

GREGGS FARISH DIED ON 7 NOVEMBER 1995 at Pointe Claire, aged 74. He was born in Brooklyn, New York to Nova Scotian parents, but subsequently went to Marlborough College before reading for an Engineering degree at the Imperial College of Science and Technology in London. His studies were cut short by the War and in April 1941, after being found unfit for flying duties, he obtained a commission in the Engineering Branch of the Royal Air Force.

In 1946 he returned to complete his degree and in 1947 he married Francesca, whom he had first met while serving in Italy. He emigrated to Canada in 1952, where he lived until his death. He had, by then, virtually completed scrutiny of the draft of the text and had selected for inclusion, a number of his own photographs.

I have been glad to accept the subsequent invitation of Francesca and her family to complete the preparation of the text and the many accompanying photographs which, with a few exceptions, were taken by Greggs at the time. In this connection, I gratefully acknowledge the assistance received from Cyril Nugent, a pre World War II member of 72 Squadron and Les Frampton, a Sergeant Pilot (later commiss- ioned) in Tunisia.   **Michael McCaul**

Preface

When No. 72 (Basutoland) Squadron received orders at Ayr in August 1942 to prepare for overseas service as a 'mobile' fighter squadron, little did either its pilots or ground staff know that by November of that year, their Squadron would be part of the first major Anglo/American amphibious operation to be launched in the European theatre in the Second World War. This expedition was given the codename 'Torch'. Its primary objective was to make landings in Morocco and Algeria. It was then to be the task of those who had landed at Algiers to drive eastwards to Tunis, to occupy Tunisia as soon as possible, and vitally, to secure airfields on the way for use by the Royal Air Force, operating in support of the land forces known as the British 1st Army, formed in July 1942.

Little did I dream, even in my wildest moments, that some fifty years later I would receive, through the good offices of Tom Hughes, an invitation to participate in the preparation, with a view to publication, of the diaries, accompanied by many photographs, which Greggs Farish was able to maintain while serving not only as Engineer Officer with 72 Squadron in French North Africa, Malta and Sicily from November 1942 to September 1943, but also with 111 Squadron in Italy from October 1943 to February 1944; after which he served with RAF maintenance units in the Naples area until receiving a Class 'B' release in April 1946.

While I knew nothing of the matter at the time, it came as no surprise to learn in 1994 that Greggs had kept such a diary in discreet but total non-observance of the rules then in force and to find that it contained such an interesting, evocative and historically valuable account of life on a mobile Spitfire squadron operating in the Mediterranean from November 1942 onwards.

Down the years, many accounts have been written about the Royal Air Force's part in Operation 'Torch' and the subsequent hard-fought campaigns in Sicily and Italy. Understandably, most have been written by, or on behalf of, the 'great and the good', or by those who bore the brunt of the battle in the air; for example *Spitfire Command* published in 1984 by the late Bobby Oxspring, who commanded 72 Squadron for most of the Tunisian campaign.

But I harbour not the slightest doubt that 'Bobby' would have been amongst the first to have applauded not only the enterprise but also the literary and photographic talents so evident in the diaries of his Engineer Officer, for these diaries provide a means, albeit belatedly, of ensuring that the efforts of the ground staff of 72 and 111 Squadrons in the Mediterranean and beyond acquire a small niche in the annals of the Royal Air Force.

Considering the strategic importance of the 'Torch' landings and the subsequent scale of defeat inflicted on the Germans and Italians in Tunisia by the Allies on the ground, at sea and in the air, there was all too little recognition of their efforts either at the time, or indeed retrospectively.

Bearing in mind not only this apparent public indifference but also the passage of time, Greggs Farish, who retired to Canada, where he would not have easy access to the relevant archives, asked me in May 1994 to contribute an introduction to his diary, and to include therein essential background with regard both to 'Torch' at the preparatory stage, and to the conduct of the subsequent campaign, with particular reference to the contribution made by the RAF formations of which 72 Squadron was a part.

Furthermore, Greggs also invited me to contribute additional information about those days which is available to me; this includes an element of personal reminiscence and will be found in Part 5. Part 6 aims to provide readers in the nineties and, hopefully, beyond, with a 'backdrop' to the participation of 72 Squadron (and 111) in a number of major amphibious landings and of the military operations after victory in Tunisia, i.e. Sicily (Husky), Salerno (Avalanche), Anzio (Shingle), Southern France (Dragoon) and North East Italy (Grapeshot).

In any event, he and I shared the hope that few of those venturing to read these pages would have been as devoid of knowledge about 'Torch' and the British 1st Army, as was regrettably an Officer at the Ministry of Defence in 1992 who, in response to an enquiry as to how the Ministry intended (if at all) to mark the 50th anniversary of the 'Torch' landings (8 November 1942), confessed readily to having no previous knowledge of either Torch or the 1st Army (as distinct from the 8th Army and the then impending 50th Anniversary of the Battle of El Alamein) and, in the light of the RAF background of the caller, ventured to suggest that perhaps 'Torch' had been merely a code name 'exclusive' to the Royal Air Force!

I offer my contributions not only as a complement to Greggs' diaries, but for what they may be worth as a belated tribute to all those with whom I had the privilege of serving in 72 Squadron in those now far off days, and not least to the author himself.

Michael McCaul

Introduction

TORCH – ALGIERS TO TUNIS

More than fifty years have passed since 'Greggs' Farish also known as 'Spanner', set down in four notebooks, his impressions of, and thoughts about, the events with which he was then concerned as an Engineer Officer in the Royal Air Force (RAF) while serving from November 1942 to April 1946 in French North Africa, Malta, Sicily and mainland Italy.

In the post-war world, and in comparison with the mass of material published about the successful Allied invasion of Normandy (Overlord) in June 1944, leading to the unconditional surrender in May 1945 of the German Armed Forces, scant attention seems to have been paid to the war in the Mediterranean, apart from the siege of Malta, the George Cross island, and the victory of the 8th Army commanded by General Bernard Montgomery (as he then was) at El Alamein in the Egyptian Desert in October 1942.

This long-awaited achievement, announced to the world on 4 November 1942, rightfully gave rise to national rejoicing at the time; but it quite overshadowed the news of large-scale Anglo-American landings in Morocco and Algiers on Sunday 8 November; this enterprise bore the codename 'Torch'.

To say the least, there is a distinct possibility that amongst those who may wish to read the diaries of Greggs Farish, there may be some who are not conversant with the background to 'Torch'. Furthermore, there may also be some who although certainly around at the time will wish to have their memories refreshed about such a daring enterprise as 'Torch', the first Anglo-American amphibious operation of World War II, and also about the course of the subsequent campaign in Tunisia, which culminated in the surrender of over a quarter of a million German and Italian troops, following the entry of the British 1st Army into Tunis on 7 May 1943.

To all those events, 72 Squadron, of which Greggs was the Engineer Officer, had its own contribution to make as part of 324 Wing.

PREPARATIONS FOR 'TORCH'

On 30 July 1942, agreement was reached that there would be an Anglo-American occupation of French North Africa (i.e. Morocco, Algiers and Tunisia, then all regarded as parts of Metropolitan France) in the autumn of 1942. This plan had borne the codename 'Gymnast' but was re-christened 'Torch', as a more inspiring name, by Winston Churchill himself. In effect, 'Torch' was to be the substitute for an American favoured plan ('Sledgehammer') which envisaged a landing in the Cherbourg peninsula in the autumn of 1942 as a preliminary to a full-scale assault on the continent in 1943. Perhaps mercifully, British objections prevailed.

'Torch' was to have an American, Lt General Dwight D. Eisenhower (then already in London as C-in-C US Forces in Europe), as its Supreme Commander, as well as a combined Anglo-American planning staff. Admiral Sir Andrew Cunningham was to be the Naval Commander of what was to materialise as a tremendous exercise of naval power, brilliantly executed by the Royal Navy, and the United States Navy, with appreciable assistance from Coastal Command of the Royal Air Force.

With regard to the possible reaction to such landings by the resident representatives of the pro-German régime in power in unoccupied France (as it then was) – led from Vichy by Marshal Pétain, Pierre Laval and Admiral Jean Darlan – it was agreed that the expedition initially be presented an all-American affair, in the not-at-all-confident hope that this might induce the French to resist less, and, after resolving their internal differences, collaborate the more with General Eisenhower.

In the event, the landings at Casablanca, Oran and Algiers cost both the Americans and the Royal Navy about five hundred lives apiece, but after an astonishing turn of events which need not be described here, Admiral Darlan, who happened to be in Algiers at the time, forsook his masters in Vichy, and emerged as the only Frenchman in North Africa then both able and willing to call a ceasefire, on 10 November, and in the six weeks prior to his assassination, to lay a foundation for collaboration with the Allied forces in all parts of French North Africa apart from Tunis; the French Resident General in Tunis in fact had lost no time after hearing of the landings on 8 November in permitting the

Luftwaffe to move in both aircraft and troops on 9 November thereby, incidentally forestalling an airborne operation against Tunis which it had been planned to launch from our newly won bases at Algiers and Oran.

At the planning stage there were differences of opinion between London and Washington both as to when and where the landings should take place (Churchill favoured October), but eventually it was decided to make landings on 8 November at Casablanca, where some 24,000 US troops (part of this large contingent later became the nucleus of the US 5th Army in Italy) would land and be prepared to move into Spanish Morocco should the Germans decide to occupy Spain. The British divisions (4th and 46th) which both later joined the 1st Army in Tunisia, were held back in the UK for similar reasons.

At Oran some 18,000 (predominately American troops embarked in the UK) would land, while at Algiers some 9,000 US and 9,000 British troops would be involved. The landings in Morocco were to be the responsibility of the US Navy, while those at Oran and Algiers were to be that of the Royal Navy, which employed some 86 warships successfully to escort 178 ships from the Clyde and Loch Ewe, to their landing points, with the loss of only a single ship.

It was to be an important part of the 'Torch' plan that on D +1 (9 November) the American assault commander in Algiers would hand over command to Lt. General Kenneth Anderson, GOC 1st Army, who would be responsible for the second phase of 'Torch' – a rapid build up of forces in Algiers as a preliminary to an advance on and occupation of, Tunisia, a fact which the planners apparently assessed as likely to take not more than 46 days (i.e. D+45=24 December). Lt. General Anderson himself had been appointed as GOC 1st Army, and military commander of the advance in Tunis, in August 1942. He replaced Lt General Bernard Montgomery, who himself had held the appointment – which he appears not to have relished – only for a day or so before being whisked off to Cairo to take command of the 8th Army. It is not without interest that Monty's own arrival in Cairo had followed closely that of General Harold Alexander, the replacement as GOC Middle East of General Auchinleck. Actually, Alexander had been the first choice as Torch's military commander and he had handed over to Monty. In February 1943, General Alexander as Commander in Chief of 18 Army Group, took under his command both Anderson's 1st Army and Montgomery's 8th Army, for the remaining weeks of the Tunisian campaign.

THE AIR PLAN

Now for the air plan for 'Torch' and the part to be played by such Squadrons as 72 and 111. Presumably because the US Army Air Force (as it was then called) was averse to serving in a unified command under an RAF Officer (and *vice versa*) there was to be no unified air command for 'Torch'. Instead there would be two separate 'geographical' commands – the Eastern Air Command (EAC) and the Western Air Command (WAC) both directly responsible to the Supreme Commander, who would have a British Air Adviser (an Air Vice Marshal) and an American Adviser on his staff. The

EAC was made up entirely of RAF squadrons, and its AOC-in-C would be Air Chief Marshal Sir William Webb (the EAC initially was referred to for security reasons as 333 Group), whereas the WAC would consist almost entirely of the aircraft of the US XIIth Air Force, some units of which had been 'blooded' in the UK since the US entry into the war in December 1941. The XIIth Air Force made use of some British aircraft, particularly the Spitfire, and on D-Day (8 November) 24 US Spitfires were to be amongst the first to land at the airfields around Oran.

In the EAC and under command of 242 Group (Air Commodore G Lawson) there were to be six RAF Wings, three of which were to be 'mobile' – 322, 324 and 325; two were to be 'non-mobile' – 323 and 328, while 326 Wing, with its Blenheim V Bisley light bombers was described as 'semi-mobile'. The three mobile Wings were all to provide air support for the advancing 1st Army, and they mustered nine Spitfire VB and four Hurricane squadrons, totalling about 200 aircraft; between them they had also had two Beaufighter night fighter squadrons and two Hurricane "Army Coopera-tion" squadrons, while 4 Photographic Reconnaissance Unit, which began its operations on D -2 from Gibraltar, was to be part of 323 Wing. Including three independent squadrons, the EAC had a strength of about 450 aircraft of all types, whereas the Western Air Command planned eventually to have some 1200 American aircraft available.

322 Wing was to be the first mobile Wing into the ring; its three Spitfire squadrons, 81, 154 and 242 (48 aircraft) were due to reach Algiers from Gibraltar on D-Day (8 November) with its Tac/R squadron (225) arriving on 12 November. On

D-Day itself the first RAF squadron to land at Algiers was 43 Hurricane squadron of 323 Wing led by the late Squadron Leader 'Mickie' Rooke.

It has been somewhat of a surprise to discover post war, that the original air plan provided for an interval of as much as fourteen days between the despatch from Gibraltar of the Spitfire squadrons of 322 Wing, and those of 324 Wing – 72, 93, 111 and 152 squadrons – on 22 November, the same day as that on which the groundstaffs of the '324' squadrons, distributed among the fifteen troop carriers contained in convoy KMF3, were themselves due to reach Algiers after leaving the Clyde on 14 November. Presumably the 'instant arrival' in Tunis on 9 November of the Luftwaffe was amongst the reasons for 111 Squadron actually being called forward to Algiers on 11 November, 93 on 13 November, 152 on 14 November and lastly, 72 Squadron (whose pilots had been in Gibraltar since 6 November) on 16 November.

The pilots of 232 and 243 forming the third mobile Wing – 325 – together with its two Hurricane squadrons – 32 and 87 – were all scheduled to reach Algiers on 6 December, the same day as their ground staffs were due in convoy KMF4. But in fact 32 and 87 squadrons did not collect their aircraft until mid-December, while 232 and 243 did not receive their Spitfires until early in January. 325 Wing's Hurricane 'Army Cooperation' (fighter bomber) squadron – 241 – actually reached Algiers on 22 November, but was not able to undertake bombing sorties until 15 December. 241 and the specialist Tac/R squadron – 225 – were the only two designated 'Army Cooperation' squadrons available to the

EAC. Later both were based at Souk el Arba along with 324 Wing.

By D +7, there were seven Spitfire and one Hurricane Tac/R squadrons available to fly in direct support of the 1st Army's advance towards Tunis, but in the preceding weeks (and indeed as was to continue to be the case at Bone for some weeks to come) the need to protect ports especially Algiers, and the mass of Allied shipping from the attention of the Luftwaffe and Italian Air Force perforce received priority.

In any event, 322 and 324 Wings could not operate as advanced mobile squadrons without access to bases appreciably nearer to Tunis than Algiers, and it was on 12 November (D +4) that the all important all-weather airfield at Bone was secured by 3–Para (who had been flown in direct from the UK since D-Day), but they were only just in time to forestall a similar German operation involving the use of JU52s. On the same day, 6 Commando were landed from two destroyers, and seized the port, while 81 Squadron as well as some Lightnings (P-38) of the WAC, moved onto the airfield there, to be joined on 15 November by 111 Squadron of 324 Wing, and by 72 Squadron on 17 November. It was at Bone that 72 scored its first success when P/O Owen Hardy shot down an Me 109.

154 Squadron of 322 Wing, to be followed by 242 Squadron, had been due to operate from the airfield at Djedjelli on 11 November and to take over the air defence of an important RN assault convoy which had been due to land troops (from the 11th and 36th Brigades of 78th Division) earlier that day (after two day's delay occasioned by bad weather) at the port of Bougie, 40 miles west of Djedjelli, where the convoy was also to land both some RAF servicing

Commandos and supplies of cased petrol for use by 154 Squadron at the airfield, already secured by Allied parachute troops. The landing of the 11th and 36th Brigade went unopposed, but at Djedjelli the landing had to be aborted because of heavy surf; the Servicing Commandos and the petrol supplies were taken back to Bougie, where the unloading of this important convoy was still in progress. But without petrol, 154 Squadron was unable to fulfil its mission to take over convoy protective duties at noon from the Hurricanes and Seafires operating from an already damaged carrier – HMS Argus, supplemented by aircraft from the auxiliary carrier, Avenger, herself then under repair off Algiers, but who had only twelve survivors when only a few days later she was torpedoed by a U-Boat and blew up while on escort duty west of Gibraltar. HMS Argus withdrew from Bougie as scheduled at noon, and in the absence of any worthwhile air cover in the area, the Luftwaffe moved in to make hay, and as a result three valuable RN ships were lost, including an A.A. ship as well as much of the gear and kit of 36th Brigade; one battalion of the Royal West Kents fought gallantly in what they stood up in for the next twenty days, unable even to effect a change of socks! From 13 November, 154 Squadron was able to operate from Djedjelli, where it was joined not only by 232, but also by 93 Squadron of 324 Wing.

OCCUPATION OF SOUK EL ARBA

On 16 November, one day late owing to bad weather, 1 Para (who had arrived in the 'Arundel Castle' on 12 November, and had expected to be 'dropped' over Tunis or Bizerta) 'dropped' instead at Souk el Arba, where they encountered no opposition in securing the grass airfield there and on to which 324 Wing, formed at Maison Blanche, Algiers on 13 November, and led so admirably by Group Captain 'Ronnie Lees' (a former CO of 72) moved without delay. By 20 November, three of the five '324' squadrons – 72, 93 and 152 – were operating from Souk el Arba; 111 Squadron did not come down from Bone until 3 December. Souk el Arba, which although 80/85 miles distant from Tunis and Bizerta, 60 miles from Tebourba, and 50 from Djebel Abiod was nevertheless the nearest Allied airfield to the 'front'.

At Bone, the three squadrons of 322 Wing as well as '111' were kept busy, lending support to the Army by protecting the port and the shipping using it to supply the advancing troops. There were numerous coastal craft and troop carriers on which both the Army and RAF had to rely for some of their reinforcements and supplies albeit on a smaller scale than would have been possible had the Royal Navy felt able to convoy larger vessels as far as Bone. The problems of re-supply in the forward areas were accentuated by the shortcomings of the French railways and a shortage of Motor Transport. Nevertheless room was found on an RN assault ship for Greggs Farish and the brand new transport of the 324 squadrons to move from Algiers to Bone on 28/29 November, and the '72' convoy reached Souk el Arba by 1 December.

The Luftwaffe made a number of determined raids on Bone, using Ju88s as well as JU 87s, Me109s and – an unwelcome sight – some FW190s. Some losses inevitably were incurred by the RAF, not least on 27 November when eleven aircraft were destroyed on the ground. Nevertheless, 322 gave a very good account of itself.

But while Bone was all weather, Souk el Arba was not, and after some spasmodic bursts of heavy rain it became a veritable mud heap. Sommerfeld tracking was laid as soon as practicable by the Royal Engineers in the face of some ground strafing, but at that time, to move by rail from Algiers sufficient tracking to lay a single runway (i.e. 2,000 tons), consumed the entire 'lift' of the railway for two days.

Even tentage was in short supply (but not tent pegs which had been packed separately!), and at Souk el Arba the Squadron's sixteen pilots slept in two bell tents borrowed from the locally based and friendly French Foreign Legion, along with some basic camp cooking equipment. Pilots not only cooked for themselves, using the excellent 'Compo' rations, but they also did their own refuelling from flimsy four-gallon tins; in Tunisia use of the "jerry can" was still a long way off. Furthermore, nothing was improved by the increasingly frequent bursts of seasonal heavy rain.

At Souk el Arba, 225 Tac/R Squadron joined 324 Wing from Bone to operate in cooperation with 78th Division, whose advance guards included elements of 11th and 36th Infantry Brigades and two composite groups known as Hart Force and Blade Force; the latter and larger group contained elements of the 6th Armoured Division, and later was effectively reinforced by a "Combined Combat" group from the US 1st Armoured Division. By 20 November, 36th Brigade and Hart Force were at Djebel Abiod, Blade Force and 1 Para (who after their 'drop' at Souk el Arba had moved up to confront German patrols near Sidi Nisr on 17/18

November using charcoal burning transport borrowed from the French Army!) were near Oued Zarga, halfway between Beja and Medjez-el-Bab (historically regarded as an invader's 'gateway to Carthage') while 11th Infantry Brigade had reached the Beja area.

No attempt will be made here to enter into a detailed account of the often fierce fighting in most difficult country in which the 1st Army found itself involved, under frequent air attack, but it deserves mention that on 24 November Blade Force and its attached US armoured units actually entered but were unable to take Djedeida, only 17 miles from Tunis, and where some JU87s were found and destroyed on the ground. Secondly, the 11th Infantry Brigade took Medjez before being repulsed at Tebourba (with heavy losses to the East Surrey and Hampshire Regiment), and the 36th Brigade's attack along the road to Mateur (and to Bizerta) was halted on 30 November after the Argyll and Sutherland Highlanders had suffered heavy losses.

On 30 November, Major General Eveleigh, the commander of 78th Division decided to "pause" for two or three days, "to await more air support" which General Anderson described as being, "insufficient for the purpose". But there was to be no "pause" for, over the next three days, the Germans mounted a series of counter attacks, closely supported by the Luftwaffe, who flew some 1684 sorties between 22 and 30 November.

Based at Souk el Arba, 72 Squadron was soon in action in support of the ground troops. Early on 21 November, David Cox, 'Pete' Fowler, 'Chas' Charnock and Les Frampton were carrying out a low level sweep east of Beja when Frampton's engine failed. He landed in a ploughed field close to a road where he was picked up by two French Officers and returned to Souk el Arba. On a late afternoon sweep on the same day the Squadron ground strafed and destroyed a German road convoy moving near Mateur. Next morning (22 November) the Squadron returned to the area, found another convoy and destroyed that also. However, Bobby Oxspring's aircraft was hit by light flak and he made a forced landing as close as possible to what he hoped was, and indeed proved to be, the British side of the front line some eight miles east of Beja. As a result he was later returned to Souk el Arba in the staff car of a most helpful but unidentified Battalion commander and after being strafed on the way, reached Souk el Arba just after one of a number of Luftwaffe raids had been made that day on the airfield, and in the course of which 72 lost seven, and other squadrons four, aircraft on the ground. It took some days to secure replacements and with 'serviceability' not usually much above 50%, it proved necessary for squadrons to pool resources to put up a credible sweep.

Nevertheless the last week of November was one of hectic activity in the air over Mateur, Djedeida and Tebourba; by the end of the month 72 Squadron had shot down nine aircraft and damaged others, including five Italian Macchis. Indeed after a month at Souk el Arba, the Squadron's score had risen to 21 confirmed and five probables; many 'claims' were substantiated by the Army on the ground. In the same period, the Squadron had lost five pilots killed, and one seriously wounded (P/O R J Robertson, subsequently awarded a DFC), and in addition to the CO, and Sgt Frampton, Warrant Officer 'Chas' Charnock who had five destroyed to his name, had 'walked home' twice after being forced to leave his damaged Spitfire in "no-man's land".

By 5 December, not only had our intrepid diarist reached Souk el Arba at the head of a convoy of 72 Squadron's twenty-three new vehicles (including a mobile office), but also a party of the Squadron's senior technicians had been flown in on a US Curtis Commando. Furthermore on 5 December itself, there arrived also the bulk of the Squadron's goundstaff as well as two pilots, led by 'Tiny' Le Petit, the indispensable Squadron Adjutant, after an eight day journey of discomfort and frustration from Algiers. Thus was the Squadron re-united for the first time since mid-October at Ouston.

This is the point when the story of 72's involvement in the Tunisian campaign may be left with advantage to the pen of Greggs Farish, augmented by the photographs he took at the time and by a number of endnotes relevant to his text and which will be found in Part 5.

Nevertheless, many things were written and said about the 'air war' in Tunisia at high levels of government and command about which those at squadron level, including our diarist, 'hadn't a clue', notwithstanding the fact that such utterances and correspondence affected and reflected (not always favourably) on what squadrons like '72' were striving to achieve often in adverse circumstances, not of their own making. Despite the passage of time, some of the issues then raised provide an interesting back-drop to the content of the diaries.

On 5 December 1942 – the same day that '72' were reunited at Souk el Arba – General Eisenhower reported to Winston Churchill that the German counter attacks of 1 to 3 December, to which the Luftwaffe had made an important contribution, had resulted in the 1st Army being driven back with 'material loss'.

As for the Allied supply resources, Eisenhower recalled that in the assault convoys, men had been given priority over equipment; thus 1st Army found itself woefully short of Motor Transport and while the railroad was being used to the maximum, sidings were congested because of a shortage of Motor Transport and "service troops". "All the native troops desert the second a bomb falls in the neighbourhood".

Surprisingly, he then gave it as his opinion that if only "we could have had in the period 15 November to 1 December, six [additional] Motor Transport Companies, this battle (for Tunis) could have been won (by now)". He went on, "Troops finally were without resources, and our aircraft were trying to support the front line from airfields 120 miles distant, whereas the enemy has to fly only 15 minutes".

Eisenhower assessed the military situation as depending "most importantly on our ability to establish fighter cover over our ground troops" — this in turn "depends on supplies, establishing forward airfields and keeping up a flow of fighter aircraft", and it was also "dependent on the weather". Another factor would be the extent to which the (continued) rapid reinforcement of the existing German force (assessed as having reached 31,000 by 5 December) could be prevented – at present our bombers were so far from their targets. Lastly he stressed the vital importance of securing continuing co-operation from the 'local' French.

In this remarkable telegram, the Supreme Commander left little room for doubt that he had been no less impressed than the British Generals Anderson and Eveleigh (78th Division) by the Luftwaffe performance in support of the German troops opposing 1st Army. In fact on 9 November, and in spite of the remarkable fact that the German High Command previously had made no contingency plan to occupy Tunisia, 27 Me109s and 24 JU 87s were drafted in, and by 15 November "Flugfuhrer" Tunisia had 81 fighters (including some FW 190s) and 28 JU 87s under command. From 1 – 3 December the 87s had flown a daily average of 54, and the fighters 128, sorties. No comparable figures for 324 Wing have been seen, although of course the RAF had no aircraft available comparable with the 'Stuka'. Nevertheless it is clear from Bobby Oxspring's book that in the last week of November, the Squadron saw hectic action on almost every mission, and that it had even gone ground-strafing at the behest of AOC 242 Group (Air Commodore G Lawson), a form of close support which was to be frowned upon by higher authority in Algiers.

Bearing in mind that between them the American Western Air Command and the EAC had at least 100 Squadrons 'on strength', it would have been difficult at that time to explain convincingly to relatively inexperienced soldiers (both British and American) why there was such a dearth of close support available, apart from 324 wing at Souk el Arba and 322 Wing at Bone. But with regard to a message sent to London by General Anderson on 2 December that he might have to consider a 'withdrawal' of his front line troops to an area where it would be less difficult for the 'air' to provide an 'air umbrella', it had been Winston Churchill himself in 1941 who had enunciated the doctrine, to the satisfaction of the RAF, that the Army (he had the 8th Army in mind) should no longer expect to rely solely on aircraft for its protection against enemy air attack, and that 'standing patrols' (i.e. an 'air umbrella') over troops were to be discontinued. A corollary to that edict was that there was always to be a sufficiency of Bofors AA guns, and 'Winston' himself already had sent 250 such weapons to Egypt. But things were different in Tunisia, since one of the many space saving decisions forced on the 1st Army in regard to the loading of the assault convoys had been to ship only a bare minimum of AA guns.

Air Chief Marshal Sir Arthur Tedder, then based in Cairo as AOC in C Middle East Air Forces (including the Desert Air Force operating in support of 8th Army) told the Chief of Air Staff in London after one of two visits he made to Algiers in December 1942, that in his view General Anderson had a "fundamental misconception" of the use and control of aircraft in "close support" and had "failed to appreciate the almost hopeless handicaps of airfields, communication, maintenance and supplies under which (Air Commodore) Lawson (242 Group of which 324 Wing was a part) had been operating." Tedder told the CAS that the RAF were in fact "doing splendidly" in Tunisia, an assessment from which there would have been no disposition to dissent at Souk el Arba!

Nevertheless there is, in retrospect, no reason to doubt that the problems confronting and giving rise to acrimony between the Army and RAF commanders would have been better addressed, if not immediately resolved, by the co-location of the operational headquarters of the EAC (Algiers) with those of 1st Army (Phillipeville), particularly as there had been no provision whatsoever made for the establishment of a rapid and secure signals link between them. Sir Arthur Tedder told CAS (and Eisenhower) how "deeply disturbed" he had been to find "non-existent inter-service channels other than the archaic French telephone system", as well as about "inadequate airfields" and that "all semblance of a combined (Air) headquarters had gone... the US XII Air Force (i.e. Western Air Command) was running a separate war".

Sir Arthur Tedder had of course, put his finger on the key point; that with a major campaign to be fought in Tunisia in 1943, there was an urgent need for a radical reorganisation of the 'air' and in January 1943 Eisenhower appointed General 'Toey' Spaatz of the US VIIIth Army Air Force as Chief of the combined North West Africa Air Force (NWAAF). Indeed later in the month, an Allied Air Support Command was set up to coordinate the operations of 242 Group with those of the newly formed US 12th Air Support Command, and with which incidentally 324 Wing was later to be closely associated in operations up to September 1944.

But at the Casablanca Conference in January, the Combined Chiefs of Staff decided to go further and in February to create a Mediterranean Air Command (Sir Arthur Tedder in command) based in Algiers, and with operational control not only of NWAAF, but also of aircraft based in Malta, and in the rest of the Middle East Air Command. The EAC and WAC were to fade away, and their many squadrons were to be redeployed in unified Allied Commands, organised on a functional basis. We need say no more here than that the Air Support Command of NWAAF became part of the North Africa Tactical Air Force (NATAF), which had under command not only 242 Group, but also the prestigious Desert Air Force, whose erstwhile Chief, Air Marshal Sir Arthur 'Mary' Coningham was to be NATAF's first Chief. Furthermore, 242 Group's new commander (Air Commodore 'Bing' Cross) also came over from the Desert Air Force, where he had led 211 Group. 242 Group, however, was to consist only of two 'mobile' wings – 322 and 324 – which between them would muster nine Spitfire Squadrons (16 aircraft per squadron), including two flying Spit 9s (i.e. 81 and 72), and one Spitfire fighter bomber Squadron (152), as well as a single Hurricane bomber Squadron (241).

The function of NATAF was to 'marshal' the much needed close support for the Armies in Tunisia, which by the end of March covered a front extending from Northern Tunisia southwards to the Libyan border, and with the Germans and Italians in occupation of the entire coastal strip. Actually in mid February, the westward thrust by Rommel's panzers through the Kasserine Pass into central Tunisia seemed for a day or so to threaten our presence at Souk el Khemis.

Frankly, and as important and far reaching as those changes were, it is recalled that at squadron level they did not cut half as much ice as, for example, a perceptible improvement in the mail service from home, popularly attributed to General Montgomery of the 8th Army then at Tripoli. Indeed what really seemed to matter more to 'the man in the squadron' was that the heavy rains should cease, as they did in late February, that additional airstrips made with Sommerfeld tracking be laid down, as indeed they were at Souk el Khemis (thanks to the sterling work of the Royal Engineers and Royal Pioneer Corps), and that the tropicalised Spitfire VB be superseded by the Spitfire IX, an aircraft which, the squadron had hopes of flying in 11 Group in the summer of 1942.

In fact 81 Squadron of 322 Wing was the first squadron in 242 Group to be re-equipped with '9s' at Gibraltar, followed closely by 72 in early February, and not 243 Squadron as some official accounts have recorded. As a footnote to the reference to 243, it was recorded that "a number of Spitfire IXs had been lying idle at Gibraltar since December 1942, and their tardy release by the Air Ministry had unnecessarily prolonged the advantage (which) the Luftwaffe had enjoyed with its FW190s". One is tempted to enquire, "With such friends, who needs enemies?"

The impact that the 9s had on the air battle over Tunisia was profound. While some of the US tactical squadrons incurred some fairly heavy losses, overall the German losses were both heavier and unsustainable, and from mid-February onwards the balance of power in the air (as distinct from the land battle) was tipping in our favour. After its 'conversion' 72 Squadron certainly did not look back in Tunisia (where it was the top scoring RAF Spitfire squadron having destroyed 53 aircraft in combat up to 13 May), or later in Malta, in Sicily, Southern France, and mainland Italy, as indeed both the diary and the additional notes on all those campaigns provided in Part 6 will confirm.

To conclude: it would be wrong to overlook the fact that after 1st Army's heroic but unsuccessful effort to reach Tunis in December 1942, five and a half months of hard fighting were to pass before General Anderson's 1st Army – which no longer consisted of just parts of 78th Division and of 6 Armoured Division (as had been the case up to the end of 1942), but by the end of April had eight complete divisions under command of its two Corps, 5th and 9th Corps, including three divisions 'on loan' from 8th Army, as well as the US IInd Corps and the French XIX Corps – scored the total victory its doggedness and valour so surely merited. Nevertheless, and as with the TORCH landings, 1st Army's success secured no real nor lasting recognition; in fact only weeks later 1st Army was dismantled and its troops were redeployed either to the 8th Army, preparing for the invasion of Sicily, or as part of the British contribution to the US 5th Army, which was to see action for the first time at Salerno. During its six month campaign in Tunisia, 1st Army suffered more than 25,000 casualties, the Americans and the French each had 10,000.

The inability of 1st Army to capture Tunis and occupy Tunisia in the forty six days apparently predicted by the TORCH planners may be said to have been offset entirely by the strategically important fact that 1st Army took some 250,000 German and Italian prisoners. It remains only to record that its victorious Commander, Lt General Sir Kenneth Anderson himself became a 'forgotten man' after his appointment to command the British 2nd Army in Normandy (Overlord) had been vetoed by General Montgomery soon after he arrived in the UK in January 1944 to become overall

Commander of all Allied land forces participating in Overlord.

The Diaries of Greggs Farish
November 1942 to April 1946

In view of my going overseas I am going to keep a Diary. The purpose of it is simply to maintain my records, in place of the letters which in corresponding with various friends and acquaintances have before given me a fairly complete record of my life in its various aspects.

Now I must prepare for a separation from all intercourse except with squadron companions which is a provision of campaigning, and since that includes, in the censorship of correspondence, the impossibility of telling of my experiences in letters to other friends in this war, I hope that telling them to myself in a diary will serve to fix them. I do not propose to write a diary by habit day by day, but just to note and describe under the appropriate date, those happenings which seem to me worth recording.

To define my present circumstances. I'm at Ouston, a 13 Group aerodrome near Newcastle, with 72 Squadron who are going overseas. I have lately joined them, leaving 222 Squadron Drem.[1]

NOTE: superscript numbers appearing throughout the text refer to the endnotes in Part 4 on page 169

All our equipment is packed in wooden cases, about 30 tons of it I suppose, waiting in the hangar. Some of our pilots have already gone including the CO Bob Oxspring who came over to 222 for the Dieppe show. We have a motley collection of Spitfires which are being disposed of one by one as the days pass. These still left are being flown a little by Americans for practice, or are simply picketed down at dispersal awaiting allotment away. There is very little to do, the whole squadron is browned off with waiting, although personally I am rather enjoying the rest and freedom from duty. We are at 12 hours readiness to embark.[2]

ON BOARD MV STAFFORDSHIRE   10-11-42

We are now on board. From Ouston I came on ahead with another officer and two NCO's to prepare to receive the men on the boat. [3]

We left Newcastle in a great rush, catching the train as it was moving. That's the second time I have nearly missed a boat train.

Mummy was on the platform. We spent the night at West Kirby and came on board next morning. West Kirby is a P.D.C. — Personnel Despatch Centre; it consists of acres and acres of wooden huts, just that.

Men sleep in dormitories, wash in a separate hut, eat in a separate hut, lounge in a separate hut. Between the huts are tarmac roads with wagons full of troops rushing up and down them, and parade grounds with men sorting out overseas kit in rows. It is a desolate man ant heap.

Liverpool, Princes Wharf (floating), MV Staffordshire, a converted Bibby Line 10,000 ton cargo liner of the 'Shires' class which used to ply between England and Burma. The crew are all Lascars, the first Indians I have met. Everybody — about 2,000 men — embarked on one day, and in the evening we pulled out into the Mersey and anchored.

Officers travel in the old 1st Class. Thus I have a cabin which I share with Van Der Veen, our cypher officer (I have the top bunk) on B Deck. Also there is a proper passenger ship's dining room and a comfortable lounge for the officers.

MV STAFFORDSHIRE   13-11-42

The ship has been converted to carry troops in the following manner. There were four holds, two in the forepart, two aft. The shafts of these holds have become stairways, with a landing every ten feet or so down. Each landing is a mess deck. Here running lengthways and stretching from one side of the ship to the other, are three banks of long tables, at which eighteen men can sit back-to-back facing the tables. There is no more room than to move your arms and legs. About 1,500 men are camped along these mess decks together with galleys, washhouses, lavatories etc. Thus below decks, the ship is a sort of hive. Sleeping is done in hammocks, stretched between beams running above the tables. Each man therefore can eat, sleep and live in a space about that in which he could stand up. If you go down to the men at night you see the floor and tables clear and then above rows of swollen hammocks, like insects in their chrysalises, swinging back and forth as the ship pitches.

In the morning, walking round the decks one comes across, on every space, men doing PT or holding classes. The decks everywhere are like a Twickenham International crowd dispersing after the match. To move from bow to stern along C deck is like moving across Piccadilly on Coronation day. There are soldiers of many different regiments, some sailors and our own airmen (who are now in khaki battledress). There are fatigue parties with brooms and shovels, there are cookhouse orderlies carrying cases of food, there are red caps and brigadiers that are hard to distinguish from privates in the throng, and there are the Lascars of the crew, like monkeys going about their jobs, rigging the life-boats or painting. There are no women at all.

After about three or four days in the Mersey we moved last night up to the Clyde; here it appears the convoy is forming. It was a fine sight coming up the estuary this morning.[4]

The sun was out, but there was a deal of mist hanging in the background. On either side was land, rising from the water's edge steeply to cliffs of 1,000 – 2,000 feet. Sometimes between the hills a waterway would turn off our main channel. East South East, behind a lower hill, could be seen the balloons and haze of Glasgow.

We passed many ships, big ones and little ones and came through a floating bar, anti-submarine and mine, which stretches right across the estuary, being opened in the middle by launches for our passage.

A baby aircraft carrier passed us, going out. We are now anchored in calm water, as are the other big ships on all sides which are also packed full of troops. Next to us is the Empress of Australia, painted dirty grey all over since Mummy and Daddy went out on it from Spain to New York. Against the grey the packed rows of khaki men with their white faces and life jackets stand out on the sloping decks. She has three funnels, we a motor vessel, have one. On the other side is one of the Union Castle line ships, good looking. There are many others, and also going between the big ships and the shore, are tugs and launches, passing perhaps on their way, a barge flying a balloon or a waiting mine sweeper.[5]

MV STAFFORDSHIRE   13-11-42 [6]

White billowy cloud, thinning to mist haze in the mountain tops. From one or two of the peaks a pennant of pure white cloud flies against the haze. Green, red, brown on the hillsides, with brilliant patches of natural colour standing out where the sun has come through the sky clouds. At the foot of the Hill, are little houses, overlooking the dark grey smooth water which is flat in the valleys between the hills. And in the foreground on the water, floating, two big ships, all grey, yet with their sharp outlines massing against the Scottish scene.

MV STAFFORDSHIRE   18-11-42

I stood, on the top main deck underneath the bridge, looking forward. Still, far away was the sky above, the white light, from a brilliant moon nearly full, showing cumulus clouds hanging in the lit back night. The moon was straight ahead of us, and high up, so that it cast its reflection on the sea in our path, which in its tossing and heaving broke the light into living silver.

And, sharp black against this film the foremast stood out, stretching upwards to where the rigging, cables and ropes, met it. This moved back and forward and from side to side across the sky in a great swaying motion. And as the ship pitched, the bows came up in solidity before the silver sea path. The forecastle was all dim light and shadows, men's shapes, rafts, two guns manned. This near world moved as the mast did, as I did, up and down, wholly, in the moonlight.

As I stood I felt the movement, my weight growing first heavy then light on my feet, and my body swaying to keep its balance on my new sea legs.

MV STAFFORDSHIRE   20-11-42

We pass Gibraltar tonight, and propose to disembark the day after tomorrow.[7] In fact we have just passed it. First the lights of a town to starboard — Tangier — and then closer yet, so you could almost see the cars, another town in Spain all lit up. Dublin was the last town I saw un-blacked-out in Christmas 1939. It was fine to see the lights. The other ships are singing, whole volumes of song floating up from the troop decks in massed chorus.

And so, in case I don't get another chance, a short description of the voyage so far. Evidently we have travelled in a big semi-circle from England to Gibraltar via the North

Atlantic. The weather has become a good deal warmer, but not hot. Rather like an English summer now. Rain and all.

The voyage has had little event. One day of rough weather. The Empress of Australia next door nearly came right out of the water pitching. Many sick, I wasn't. Fourteen or fifteen troop ships in the convoy. Eleven destroyers and corvettes I counted this morning dropping depth charges ahead. But no torpedoes, although some porpoises. One man fell overboard off another ship and was rescued by a corvette. Occasional aircraft have circled us, Sunderlands and Catalinas. Today we nearly had a prang in broad sunlight, our ship forgetting to go about when the rest of the convoy did, tacking.

I have spent my time sleeping, reading, writing, playing chess, poker and draughts a little, eating, but mostly sleeping. I have read "Rough Justice" by C E Montague, some of Cowper's letters, "Reveille in Washington" by Margaret Leach and a marvellous book "The Importance of Living" by Lin Yutang, which I have also spent some time reviewing; though not yet finished. I have visited the engine room — 16 cylinder Diesel with two 4-cylinder Diesel-Electric plants, etc. I have been in charge of a boat muster station of about 80 men. I am rested by the voyage and by the amount of sleep I have been getting; must have needed it.

We have seen nothing of the enemy.

ALGIERS   22-11-42

We arrived here this morning. As I am writing, I am sitting perched up on some wooden supports above the top deck.

The sun is bright in a clear light blue transparent sky, with wisps of cloud high up here and there. Below me a gramophone is singing "Star Dust".[8] The view — well I suppose I had better try and describe it. Hills, dry brown and with some green woods. Below the sky line right down to the sea, white blocks of houses, white in terraces, with the sun reflecting off them. And then the smooth sea, emerald blue vivid colour. And all around ships, destroyers, cargo boats, passenger steamers, boats. In-shore there is a bright red buoy, standing out against the blue sea and white houses. There is a breeze blowing. On top of the hills in one place there is a needle monument.

There seems to be no one, no cars nor people or movement in Algiers, except semaphore or Aldis signals; and occasionally a destroyer comes up alongside and yells directions. We are moving slowly in, past the other ships.

BONE   28-11-42

Well, I shall have to be short. A great deal has happened, some marvellous times, some adventures, some tours, in this South coast of the Mediterranean. We were three or four days encamped on a road, — just myself and 25 MT drivers — on the coast near Algiers. Then we moved by boat, a Royal Navy assault ship, up the Mediterranean to Bone.

Smooth, quiet, exceptional passage. Two days here assembling and loading our vehicles, going full tilt, and tomorrow morning I'm going on with most of them in convoy to the aerodrome up at the Tunisian front.

At Algiers... and here we have been blitzed regularly at night and occasionally bombed by day as we move up the lines of communication.

I am getting used to it, and learning how to take cover quickly, under the nearest lorry. We lived there right on the beach in a sort of water-level pumping station for the electricity works. It was warm, lit, safe and dry until a high tide flooded us out on the third night when we just dispersed into Algiers town.[9]

The town itself I was surprised at. It was really fine, the shops, the terraced buildings, the roads, the architecture, the courteous people, French and Arab, the smart women, the sun on street cafés, the typical French trams, and the bigness of it. Points to note:- The very good French re-construction and civil engineering works going on, the cleanliness, the tropical trees, the new Government buildings, the Post Office, the mosques, the wide streets and the harbour. I have photographs of it, and some postcards.

When passing the Post Office an idea struck. It seemed to be in good civilian working order so I strolled in, uniform and all and was able to send a cable to my mother in England. "Arrived safely." This would have Algiers marked on it and was sent at least eleven days after the original landing by the Torch invasion forces. The cable got through safely!

I am tired of sitting among my blokes with Richardson who joined me from the rest of the squadron before we left Algiers and has been a great help here. We all are singing and Cpl. Iddendon is playing the piano.

We are all living in a house we have found. Furnished and set pink-walled in a small garden of orange and lemon trees.

Indeed the owners must have left it in a hurry, — unwashed dishes on the kitchen table — and must be fairly well off. When I got up this morning and went out on the porch in the rising sun, I beheld the blue Mediterranean and to the left the coastline curving across the green bay, with the mountains behind. It was beautiful, just one of many beautiful parts of this world. All day we have been working with the lorries in the warm sun, on this road by the sea.

We sleep in blankets on anything, never take our clothes off. We eat tinned food, "Compo Rations" very good, cook it ourselves. We drink from our water bottles. We have finished the voyage by sea, and now go on by road.

SOUK EL ARBA   10-12-42 [10]

To describe the long drive up here from Bone. About 200 miles. It took us a day and a half, with three ton lorries towing trailers in convoy. For the first quarter we drove inland across a plain as the sun rose. Through Duviviers and climbed up slowly in brown hilly country, dry, dusty, barren, with sudden wide views back down the brown valleys as you came round a curve, to Souk Ahras. Near there I called in at a "Command Post" and was congratulated on the speed with which we had got cracking, and warned against being strafed when we got down on to the plain, the other side of the mountains. From Souk Ahras we wound down the side of the hill, passing for about two hours an American tank division standing on the road in the heat of the noonday sun. It was very hot, and dusty. At one hairpin I waved an American "half truck" over so that we could pass. I was hailed: "Say Tommy, keep off the roads. We gotter win this war for yer!" Now our Intelligence say that an American tank division — part of a 'Blade Force' — has been annihilated.

We pushed on, three 3-tonners, one Coles Crane, one Firetender, one Ambulance, one Petrol tanker, two 30 cwts and a Humber brake, up a long climb into the mountains. The road wound like a snake, there was much traffic — lorries, tanks, motor cyclists, all going forward. We climbed slowly higher and higher, it grew cooler, more barren, as the shadows lengthened. Solitary Arabs watched the stream from the hillsides, sinisterly.

It became endurance, just pushing on. One of the 3-tonners broke down but caught us up by night-fall. We reached the top about 5 o'clock or so, a lonely fork in the road at 2,500 feet. As we descended night fell and we just stopped, cooked a meal and went to sleep until dawn. Then we pushed on, mostly down hill this time, a little more green among the everlasting brown, until suddenly we saw the plain below us, stretching brown flat between hills on either side. We spread out then, and our speed increased so that we became a long caravan, each vehicle half a mile apart with its train cloud of dust moving across the dry brown plain in a straight line. We arrive at Souk el Arba in time for dinner which we cooked ourselves as ever. [11]

I was the first man of the squadron to arrive here having come by land and sea. Today, eleven days later 90 more men have come in, and yet there are still more to come. When I got here I found eighteen or so of the pilots in a French tent on the end of a telephone line and with a trench nearby. On the other side of the road was a conglomeration of aeroplanes all over the aerodrome, and among them, here and there, a pile of empty petrol tins in the dust with, around these, men in tattered bits of uniform, dirty, long haired, unshaven, tools sticking out of their pockets, cooking food over fires among the 'planes or dashing out to service aircraft as they landed.

These were the RAF "Commando" servicing echelon, the same as Becker's lot which I met at Ipswich. Two flights of them, about 200 men I suppose, keeping flying four squadrons of Spitfires, one of Beaufighters some Hurricanes and occasionally a squadron of Bisleys visiting. They came in with the original assault and today are preparing to move out now that the squadron's personnel are coming up. In my opinion they have done a damn fine job and I wish I was with them. The men are different from the average RAF airman. Much more independent and "don't care a damn who you are" sort of attitude. They are all Fitter II's. They are tough too. I like working with them.

The first few days it was hot and sunny, yet cold at nights; we were working in our short sleeves at noon. It is winter here now. In the sun perhaps an airman would be having a bath on the perimeter track, standing nude beside a petrol can. One day I decided to have a crack at moving a Potez, French twin-engined medium bomber about the size of a Boston, which was lying on its belly in the middle of the 'drome, had been for several days. There were three 3½-ton mobile cranes on the station by this time and we lifted it, one on each propeller, and one backward on the tail. Thus, clear of the ground and suspended by the three identical cranes, the Potez moved slowly across the aerodrome, a queer sight with the three crane jibs stretching up in the gathering dusk. It was difficult to coordinate the movements of the cranes both in lifting; neither one must take more weight than the other as you lift, and in moving; neither one must move faster or in a different direction from the others. It was a most interesting lift. I think I could have won several bets on it. My own theory is that if you have got enough power you can move big things as easily as you can move little things by your own limbs. The art of using mechanical power lies in knowing what is going to break first, the jibs or gravity, the rope or the mud, the bit or the metal.

A few days after I had been here W/O Norton, Armourer, F/Sgt. Landon, i/c B Flight and Sgt. North, Fitter II, dropped in by air with about 30 men.

More bodies to muck in and this was the first of the change-over from Commando maintenance to squadron maintenance which is still going on.

The above three joined me in a tent. One day we decided not to go down to the cookhouse for dinner; we reckoned we could do better ourselves. So we first put some water in a biscuit tin and some tins of stew and rice-pudding in the water and sat round inside the tent smoking, or shaving, waiting for the water to boil. It did, was boiling away merrily when all of a sudden it caught alight. "All right it's only some petrol on top of the water from the tin. I should think the food's hot enough anyway." So we took the tins out, and by adroitly lifting it on a spade handle we got the blazing water out of the tent. We opened the tins of food. The blaze outside was increasing. "Must have been a hell of a lot of petrol in that water." We tasted the food. Paraffin, completely spoilt. We had boiled it in paraffin instead of water. It was, by now, too late to go down to the cookhouse.

The ground is crumbly and cracked earth, brown with cracks and holes in it from the heat. It was cultivated land and I couldn't see how anything could grow on it. The earth is good and deep, being situated on a plain with mountains all round, and there are two rivers rather sparse and muddy on either side of us, but it was very dry.

We pitched our tents, on the flat ground, and the earth became the floor of our house, the sky the ceiling. Then came the rain. It rained for a whole night and day, and drizzled for a few more days. And we were, of course flooded out. The mud was universal. Walking became like ploughing. The aircraft were all bogged. No transport, except the four-wheel drive 3-tonners, could move. My motor bike got stuck in the mud.

We had water 6" deep inside the tent. My 'grave', for sleeping in to eliminate having to go to the slit trench during night bombing, became a lake, and we were all wet through with no hope of getting dry. Camping lost its romance all of a sudden like. But now it has cleared up again, and although cold at night, it is sunny and warm when the wind is low in the daytime.

You can see by the gap how I have been working. I got my first bath since being in North Africa, yesterday. One month and three days with only the rain to cleanse. Most of the squadrons have had mail now, but I haven't except for an invitation to attend a meeting of the I.Mech.E. to discuss "Steam raising by coal". Tea will be served at 5 pm! In Manchester! That arrived on 17/12/42. My first letter!

I wish I would get some mail. All day and all night I am among the aeroplanes and mud. The C.O. and all the pilots live mostly in the air or in bed, but I stay always with the aeroplanes. Take today. This morning at breakfast I arranged for a lorry to go to Ghademou for blankets and torch batteries. Then three kites got stuck in the mud landing after a sweep. Got those debogged and back to their wire hard standings. V's aileron had been smashed by another kite of 152 Squadron taxiing into it at the end of the runway. Then 'Tiny' appeared, an hour late for his pay parade. Nobody turned up for it because we were all too busy on the aerodrome. There was another show to take off at 1.30 pm. Re-fuel, re-arm. Tiny was mad. "Alright, damn them, if they don't want pay, they won't get it". I soothed him and persuaded him to take the trouble to go round the flights to each section instead of the usual admin. method of knocking everybody off work to queue up all morning. I organized that with the sections then, cursing and blinding at any bodies who came, as they do, out of place. "Go on, clear out, this is B Flight, not the orderly room, you'll be paid later — what the hell are you doing here, get out, let's have some order round here, those kites have got to take off," etc. etc. Then people came worrying about the Commandos' armament stuff which they left behind when they left and now claimed I had lost! I escaped to lunch. There met Smith back from Ghademou with no cooking burners, so sent him off again to look for them at Wing Stores instead; and dealt with an ACH who got drunk while cleaning up after a pilot's party, one morning and was 'out' all day. Sent him back to base, with recommendation for leniency as he didn't know what whisky was, after a severe lecture on trust and conditions in the field, etc.

Then over to B Flight on my motor bike and discovered them about to push 'V' up after changing the aileron by a rigger who had never seen a Spitfire aileron before and, of course, had got the droop wrong. Worked with him and taught him how to do it until it was right and left him to lock up and sign up. Talked to Peter Fowler (pilot) about air testing ailerons for ride-up at 400 mph. Dispatch Rider came back from Webster (OC Commando's) with a note about "what about his starter trolleys". Had already arranged with W/O Weedon to get them loaded on the 'artic' and back. Arranged one or two details with Tiny before he left. Another DR arrived with plugs sent for from echelon at base. Good. Moans about the food in the 'flights' so at tea told the cooks to give everyone as much as they wanted and that a cook must go round to the flights, with the food to hear if there were any complaints as he dished out. After tea got the day's returns in; "15 serviceable, one repairable on site, two awaiting spares, 1,100 gallons of petrol used." Bloody good, best of the squadrons, in a good temper therefore. Talking to Sgt. Blackie in A Flight about G, suggested we look at engine controls before we changed the plugs, so we took out a truck, found the kite in the dark, and confirmed my suspicion that they were all out. Spent an hour readjusting these, going over the boost control, datum lines, a frame throttle rod, solo running, mags. Ran the Spitfire up in the dark — flaming exhausts cockpit lit up from the reflector sight — readjusted the boost at the gate, then made him run it up and it was perfect. Then down to the school to see F/Sgt. Horner who had come up from base with some stores and fixed up four Americans who had crashed in a Fortress, to go back with him. That's about all. Haven't washed today after my Turkish bath last night.

A good day, plenty of flying, the aircraft taking off through a water-shoot and mud all down the runway. Marvellous sight. Blokes happy. No bombs yet though Jerry was over in the morning. Cold, almost English winter, cloudy, windy.

The squadron is now split in two halves. Servicing Flights, pilots and Engineer and Intelligence Officers, forward; echelon, clerks etc. and Adjutant Medical Officer based back at Ghademou with whole of wing HQ.[12] Thus we are now mobile (my old dream) and it is working well. We can move complete, men, tents, rations, equipment, petrol, ammo. at short notice quickly in fifteen 3-ton lorries and trailers and vans, car, ambulance etc.

SOUK EL ARBA   29-12-42

Some fifteen days ago I saw ten Bisleys take off, of 18 Squadron, after we had refuelled them on a daylight bombing raid. None came back.[13] It appears that there was an enemy tank concentration somewhere behind Medjez el Bab, which was a very serious threat to the Army's already precarious positions. So the RAF called on light bombers, which came up from the Algiers area for the job. When they arrived at Souk it was found impossible, due to our being blitzed, to give them any fighter cover. The show was therefore cancelled, but their CO, W/C Malcolm, understanding the Army's predicament, volunteered to try and get through on their own, knowing the opposition strength and the obsolescent type of aircraft 18 Squadron were flying. They did not have the luck of the Gods, and when they were spotted by a flock of 109's were all shot down, one by one, by the aerial flying squad.

Note later: I believe three crews survived. Malcolm got a posthumous VC and there came out of this do, one of the best RAF institutions overseas, — his wife formed, in his memory, the "Malcolm Club", which became the airman's own private paradise all over the Mediterranean theatre.

EXTRACT FROM A LETTER HOME   30-12-42

What out of? Mud, mountains, slow sliding rivers; out of aeroplanes and Arabs; out of the moans of the camp guard, and the hopes of the married men; out of avions and ships and kites. Out of slit trenches and bombholes and tents. Out of brown men, many of them, and especially out of flight, diving, climbing, banking, soaring, and out of crashes, nosed-over, landed wheels up, overshot, spun in, shot down in flames. Out of the blue sky, the wispy clouds, the black puffs of ack-ack fire; and the red tracer shells moving. Out of wet clothes and cold food, out of healthy bodies and alert faces. Out of the sound of many voices singing the old songs in the evening time, and the rising full-clothed from wet blankets in the morning. Out of the return of missing pilots and the wait for mail. But above all, out of the sun flash of a Spitfire weaving.

SOUK EL ARBA   1-1-43

At Souk, about this time, 152 Squadron cracked up and had to be pulled out to Constantine. It happened like this. The original "152" was lost at Singapore. A new squadron was formed somewhere in the North of England for the North African invasion. The CO, Flight Commanders and one F/O were about the only pilots with 11 Group experience. Just after they reached Souk I think, their CO went sick. Then, in the intense fighting against superior odds, one flight commander bought it and the other was wounded. the F/O was leading the squadron, and of course, having no experienced blokes with him, they lost a lot from their formations. The Army advance had been halted and they found they had a trifle over-reached themselves. The Army were screaming very forcibly that the cause was lack of air support, and they were being continually dive-bombed. The whole wing had become so pushed that out of the four squadrons we were often lucky if we could twelve-up altogether on patrol.

The wily Hun knew this and used to wait until our blokes had been on patrol for an hour, knowing they had no more fuel, and would then seize his opportunities. He was using Me 109 Gs (superior aircraft to our Spit. VBs), FW 190s, and even Ju 87s, so secure did he feel. We were on an aerodrome that was rapidly becoming a mud swamp, and he was operating from such places as the straight wide tarmac road which runs between Tunis and Carthage. '72' having XI Group experience and Bobby Oxspring leading them — throughout the campaign never lost any of his sprog tail-end Charlies — or very few — two or three since the assault actually killed, although two went 'round the bend' and several were wounded — kept on steadily scoring. III Squadron also with XI Group experience, were scoring the same but were losing more. '93' Squadron recently re-formed like '152', lost a lot of pilots and shot down few. 152's morale, with no leaders, was going.

Then there came a day when six Spits were sent forward to an advanced landing ground at Medjez el Bab on the Army's insistence. It was a suicidal venture and everybody knew it. I remember the tension at the Group Captain's conference the night before, when Squadron Commanders drew lots for the job. The strip was just about within range of the enemy's machine guns. '93' and '152' lost and had to send three each. Of 152's three, two were shot down on take-off from Medjez by Hun ground gunners.

There was no radio-location yet organized to speak of, and since we ourselves were losing so many kites on the ground, from the Hun dive-bombing without warning, it had been arranged for there always to be an aerodrome patrol of two Spits above us. That same day '109's came over, bombed and shot down both the two Spits, over their own 'drome. I watched them coming down. Nothing is more disheartening. '152' had been on patrol at the time.[14] That finished '152'; the remains of the squadron had to be withdrawn. Finally just to top off their run of bad luck, a train came along at a level crossing on the way back to Constantine and wrote off one of their lorries filled with ground crew, including their W/O Armourer!

(I must add that some months later '152' came back to Khemis, joined 322 Wing, and under their same original Squadron leader, did very well, including knocking up 322 Wing's top score in Malta. This case is the only one I know of a Squadron's morale going — though I believe it nearly happened to '72' in the Battle of Britain.)

SOUK EL ARBA   6-1-43

It rained all Christmas eve and Christmas day.[15] Our tents were inundated with mud, our aircraft were bogged, our clothes were wet through. We got no mail, no extra food, no drink. A more wretched Christmas day I cannot imagine. And yet in spite of our thoughts of home and family and of our desolate activity, we had Christmas cheer.

On Christmas eve we heard that some NAAFI stores had arrived to set up shop in the village of Souk el Arba. So, W/O Norton and myself grabbed a lorry and went off to do a little scrounging for the boys. We found the dump in a back yard. Moonlight night. No guard seemed to be about. So quickly in the back of our wagon we heaved four cases of 48 bottles of BEER in each. We got away with it.

Next morning, just to start off a merry Christmas, the last two petrol stoves in the cookhouse trailer packed in. The rain made cooking outside difficult. So we just distributed boxes of Compo-rations — one per 14 men was the official scale — one to each tent, and a bottle of beer to each man. Most people spent Christmas day half in bed to keep warm and everybody had a good feed and drink.

On boxing day I went down to the NAAFI and saw the Sergeant about the beer. "Criminal offence, stealing rations" he said, "but still it isn't everybody that comes back and pays for it afterwards". So the matter was settled.

Several times recently we have been attacked from the air in daylight. Once I had just said "Good bye" to Lou Costello, Martin and Jo Ekberry (old members of 222) who had dropped in for an hour in a Dakota and had been shooting the hell of a line about air raids etc. when an attack developed. I dived into a gun pit. There were some Hun fighters high up in the blue sky. Our aerodrome patrol was up and a marvellous dog-fight ensued. A Spit shot down and the Me 109's got away. That must have shaken old Lou.

Next at tea time with no warning at all there was suddenly a terrific roar over our heads, bullets and cannon shells whizzing about and then three or four loud bangs as the bombs dropped. Right by the echelon. One of the fitters was adjusting the C/S Unit on 'A'. A piece of shrapnel smashed the engine beside his hands. Then he dived underneath the lorry, having no time to get to a slit trench. Another bomb went off, a splinter caught the front tyre, and the lorry descended over him with a hiss! For days after that I had a job to keep the echelon from diving into the trench at the sound of an aeroplane engine.

The third effort shook me. I was out in the middle of the aerodrome with the crane salvaging 'V' which Sgt. Sollitt had turned over on its back landing. The sun was out in a clear sky and the crane's jib was up for the lift. Suddenly ack-ack fire opened up; looking towards the black puffs we saw seven or eight Hun fighter bombers coming across the sky. I just stood and looked, most interested, studying the formation shapes, number, and noticed how the sun glinted on them. Strange aircraft.

Then they peeled off right over our heads and dived slightly, loosing bombs. I also dived underneath the crane, and watched a silvery bomb coming down. I knew it was going to miss us — it landed near 'A' Flight, damaging two Spits. Series of terrific explosions. Great columns of earth sprang up on both sides of us and in front. A Beaufighter at the end of the runway quite near, burst into flames. I thought what a place to be, in the middle of the aerodrome with a pranged kite and a great crane.

It was all over. Bombs had landed all round us. The Beaufighter burnt to a carcass. One of the Huns was shot down by the aerodrome patrol.

So it goes on. Every day or so we get a small raid, suddenly. We learn to know where is the nearest slit trench, always.

Today a queer thing happened. Due to the mud causing aircraft to go up on their noses so often, the Group Captain has ordered that when taxiing, an airman must always sit on the tail.

In the hurry of a "scramble" one of 'III's pilots forgot all about his airman when he turned onto the strip and opened up with the airman still on the tail. The poor bloke must have been too frightened to fall off as the Spitfire gathered speed and the next thing they were airborne. Imagine the pilot's consternation when he, unable to trim the aircraft, looked in the mirror and saw an airman waving in the breeze round his rudder! He managed to stagger round the circuit on full power, and mushing like hell, while the terrified man hung on like grim death. In the belly landing the airman was thrown clear, and broke his leg. That was all.[16]

EXTRACT FROM A LETTER TO SQ/LDR CHAPMAN   21-1-43

For instance, one dusk we got dive-bombed and several aircraft were destroyed. So the next evening the CO told the pilots to disperse aircraft at the end of the day's flying, in another field. It rained all that night, and by morning we had eight kites bogged up to the axles. Tried everything to move them, full throttle with men on the tail and underneath the wings, towing with a four-wheel drive heavy lorry, laying wire tracking down in front of them, etc., but they just sunk further into the mire. Until finally we got our 3-ton Coles crane out, took a lift straight on the prop (!) and dragged them upwards and out.

Again an aeroplane landed wheels first into a mud patch, and so went over on its back. It was in the way so we just borrowed a Bulldozer from the Royal Engineers and shovelled it off the runway. You have never seen so many wrecks in your life as there were on our first aerodrome (so called) after a month's operations and before the salvage unit arrived in the area. Nor so much flying. Every aircraft there was, which could take off, flew. Four and five times a day on sweeps. The Wing would start off in the morning putting fourteen up. By dinner time it would be down to ten, and even if we only had two left, still they would be off on a last sweep. Replacements would arrive perhaps, — no allotments, in fact it was a case of which squadron they happened to taxi over to as to which adopted them, — and the acceptance check consisted of refuelling and chalking a letter on its side before it took off on operations!

No such thing as a Form 700 in those days . . . . and when he (pilot) landed again, he made damn sure it was refuelled and rearmed, himself ... else he might run out of fuel on the next trip, which did happen on one occasion. — Twice in one day I got complaints of oil pressure dropping off in flight. On investigation I found it was due to there being no oil in the tanks. Some of those planes flew 30 or 40 hours without a daily inspection, without even taking the cowlings off.

Now of course, it is not like that at all ...

Not long after my last entry more rains came and we were wallowing around bogged kites in the mud. Meanwhile a new strip had been laid down (strip of wire mesh unrolled called 'Somerfeld' tracking) at Souk el Khemis about twelve miles forward.[17] Therefore one morning our aircraft took off and landed after a sweep on the new landing ground. We on the ground were then informed that the squadron had moved temporarily, and soon got mobile. The flights went forward, leaving skeleton crews behind to clear up, the equipment and NCO's of the echelon came up to Arba from Ghademou. Then the remainder of the men and aircraft got away from Arba and again the flights moved to another new strip way, forward again about three miles which we were to share there with 241 Squadron, Army Co-op. For about a week in a state of flux, moving and yet flying the aircraft. It was the first time we had tested our mobility and I was much pleased how well the different section's moves coincided and the aircraft were kept flying to the end when we were all on our new aerodrome in working order. We arrived and the kites landed on the strip as the Pioneers and RE's finished it in the evening light.

Coxie in 'B' and Pete Fowler in 'Q' had landed and taxied off when I saw 'E' going round the circuit a second time waggling his wings. I watched him for a bit, thinking his undercarriage might be stuck up. Then I ran across to 'Q', asked Pete who it was and what his call sign was.

It was Sexton Gear, a pilot of over 1,000 hours Spit experience which is a good thing on these occasions. I called him up on the R/T, sitting in Pete's cockpit on the ground.

"Hallo Fetter Blue 2, this is 'Spanner' calling, can you hear me?"

He answered in his gruff voice. "Hallo Spanner", rather pleased and surprised; "I can't get the undercart selector lever down, it's stuck about half-way, can I use the CO_2 Bottle?"

I told him no, his locking pins were jammed, that it was no good waggling his wings and diving, for the legs were still locked up and what he wanted was negative 'g' so to try flying on his back. At which he climbed to a considerable height, turned over on his back and flew like that until flame spurted from the inverted engine.

Next thing on the radio, "OK Spanner, I've got 'em down, thanks very much". He landed safely.

The squadron lives here at a farm about two miles away from the aerodrome between the feet of the mountains on one side and a railway single line on the other. It is pleasant. The officers have a sort of bungalow for a mess. There is a Sergeants' mess in a marquee and an Airmen's mess in a cowshed, we have pigs meandering round our tents, children wandering about, Italians, French, and Arabs living among us. We are still in tents, but the weather daily becomes warmer and there is not so much rain, although of course the farm abounds in shit, literally.

The aerodrome is paradise compared with Souk el Arba, it is on sandy soil covered with green grass — green at this time of year — it is not dead flat, there is a farm to one side of it, amongst whose hay stacks my echelon is lodged, complete with bus — mobile workshops — and hard standings for the aeroplanes here and there. The ground is easy to dig and porous so that little water stays on top and there is no longer mud. We have sunken some of our tents, covered others to look like hay stacks, we have a wide dispersal with each Spit on its own hard standing and a thin winding perimeter track to the runway end. There are telephones between the dispersed tents, and I think the whole thing is so well organized that I can leave the maintenance of aircraft to run itself. Or so it has seemed these last few days.

Since we moved we have not been blitzed, nor I think found by the Hun, and there has not been so much flying on our part, so that we have been able to introduce 80 hour inspections, and we have cleaned up the Spit's lines, between flights, filing off here, filling there, spraying and painting here, patching smooth there, so that they are beautiful now. We have put the squadron's marking on them, which in the assault we were not allowed to wear, the famous 'RN'. And we have been working in the sun all day long. It has become more like XI Group last summer now, for the time being two or three sweeps a day, putting whole squadrons up. Today we put fifteen up at once on one sweep.

On the wall of our small mess there are stuck up two photographs from old newspapers. I think they just about represent all our hopes and aspirations. One is a lurid pose of Betty Grable, and the other is a Spitfire IX. Now the news has come through that 72 Squadron is to move temporarily to Constantine to re-equip. So both our hopes may, after all, be realized.

Two days ago, among the many aircraft turning round the sky above the two aerodromes I saw one spinning down with one wing sliced off. It hit the ground, exploded, and when we got to it the pilot and engine were about 14 ft deep. 109's about? But no, looking up again there was another Spit spinning out of control and then a blob separated from it at about 1,000 ft, and a parachute opened. It was the 'Wingco' himself (Gilroy) cut in the face and much shaken from the collision and such a low jump. That was the second collision we had in one week.

One day Arthur Richardson and I planned the mounting of a gun in the back of one of our light Bedfords. We thought it would be useful in convoys and for going up to the front line if necessary, because many lorries have been destroyed on the roads by enemy aircraft so that now we always have a look-out on the roof. So a fine pair of Browning machine guns were erected in the back of the van. 'Tiny' then happened to take the van to advanced 5 Corps Army HQ. He drove in the yard majestically, shooting quite a line with the gun in the back, swung round to park and gun and gunner fell out "coblunk" at the mansion steps astonishing various Generals and giving great amusement to the "Brown jobs". The mounting had been bolted securely to the floor boards all right, but unfortunately, to that part of them where there was an inspection panel for the back axle.

243 Squadron has come into this 'drome from England. I met Engineer Officer Broughton whom I last saw leaving Drem for Hornchurch with 453. Very surprised and glad to see them. Also met Cpls Monks, O'Connor and Chadwick from 222.

72 Squadron is the crack squadron in this campaign, our score being top at 31 so far.

CONSTANTINE   3-2-43

The Squadron is being re-equipped with Spit IX's.[18] Therefore all the pilots have come back to Constantine, and are at 24 hrs notice to move to Gibraltar to collect the new aircraft. Arthur Richardson and I have come with them for a few days rest. We came by motor cycle, the trip taking us two days of mishaps. My petrol tank cracked open underneath at a seam and petrol was sprayed on my legs for several miles which later caused grievous irritation for a few hours. We spent almost all the first afternoon getting that repaired by REME. We made Souk Ahras the first night and there stayed in a clean hotel and dined in state.

Next day we went on through the mountains, taking the wrong road at one point, of which we were the more glad because between Souk Ahras and Ain Seymour we passed through some marvellous country; mountains, trees, rocks, fields, chalets; it seemed like Switzerland in summertime. We stopped at 108 Repair and Service Unit, Duvivier, for lunch; I hoped to see Gesswell and F/S Barlow but they were at Bone. We carried on well until before Guelma, when Richardson's back tyre went flat due to a tin opener punc-turing it. Directly after that my clutch cable broke, so we were both stuck. We thought we had it for that day then, but we found an RASC workshop in Guelma, got both bikes repaired and decided to try and make Constantine before dark. There was about 2½ hours daylight and 114 kilometres left to go. We made it in 1_ hours, that last stretch racing each other all the way and averaging 43 mph. We then spent another 1_ hours finding "L'École d'Industrie" where the pilots and us were to put up. That was exasperating.

CONSTANTINE 17-2-43

I was talking to a pilot of 242 Squadron, in the Casino this morning, over a cup of coffee. He was back for a rest, awaiting posting to non-op flying so I asked him why, and this is what he told me.

"I have had some adventures in the few months I have been out here, and I have had about enough. First, two days after we got here I was shot down off Bone and had to bail out over the sea. I was rescued by a ship after paddling about in my dinghy for an hour or two.

"Not long after that seven of us took off on a sweep. After about half an hour's flying my engine cut out over enemy territory, due to the petrol filters being choked. I left the formation and tried to get home pumping petrol into the engine with the throttle and kigass pump. All the way I was looking for landing ground in the mountains but I just managed it. But it was just as well my engine cut because of the seven which took off on that show, only one other came back besides me, and he was shot to hell. Another pilot walked back. Don't know what happened to the other four.

"Then I got captured. Yes. Shot down again and crash landed among a crowd of Jerries. It was an infantry detachment, cut off and retreating. I was with them two days up in the hills without anything to eat. They had good equipment and were all on foot. I thought of making a break for it but am glad I didn't now, there wasn't a chance with their machine guns. They took my revolver. Nothing else. The Oberlieutenant was a fool. I pretended I had malaria, shivered all one night, it was not difficult with the cold, and suggested to them malaria, which was confirmed by their medical orderly. No doctor. And I spun them a yarn about the British surrounding and still advancing so that they decided to go, and I couldn't move, so they had to leave me. As soon as they were out of sight round the hill though, I moved like hell and got across the lines disguised as an Arab with a blanket over my head.

"After that my first trip was to flight-test a repaired kite. It crashed on take off. The fuselage was twisted. That shook me and I got sinus trouble so they sent me back."

He didn't say how many Huns he had shot down and I didn't ask him.

ADDITION TO DIARY MADE AT SORRENTO   22-2-45

There were two other pilots' stories worth remembering of those days at Souk el Arba/Souk el Khemis. First of Charles Charnock — "Chas" to 72.[19] If ever you saw a dissolute looking fellow, here was one. W/O Charnock, DFM, who even in his worn flying clothing, one felt would be better placed propping up a night club bar. At least he usually contrived to have a bottle of whisky in his hand when on the ground. He was over 30, far the oldest pilot in the squadron; a regular, and before the war had been a substantive Flight Lieutenant, until he pushed a senior officer into a fishpond. He had flown everything and had broken Spitfires up in the air with aerobatics. He was the maddest fighter pilot I ever met, completely round the bend; — and yet one felt he had seen the whole world. Perhaps he had, and in his wisdom, found only flying left. And he flew only to kill and be killed.

In the early days, at Algiers and Bone and Souk, he knocked three down in no time at all. Also he got shot down himself twice, and it was one of his first bar stories how he had persuaded the Air Force that he had baled out, complete with all his kit in a kit bag, for compensation.[20] Twice he had pocketed the gold sovereigns of a pilot emergency wallet. The second time he had descended into no-mans land and, meeting an Arab with a donkey, tried to borrow the transport. But the Arab would not play, so Chas pulled out his revolver and shot a stray dog passing by, dead. He then had no difficulty in riding home on the Arab's donkey.

Then naturally came the day when Chas was missing again. This time believed killed. Last seen, he had broken away from Bobby Oxspring's formation, straight into a gaggle of Huns up sun, alone. No news for two days. Then a signal came in from an Army Casualty Clearing Station, "Credit me with two. Chas." He got the DFC after that.

He was seriously injured in the crash. And didn't fly again for two months after which time he turned up from Algiers with a medical certificate OK. 5,000 ft over Khemis caused him to pass out in the cockpit and when he got down again they found the medical chit was forged. He was promptly sent back to base and from there to UK.

That is only a small part of his whole story which he alone could tell of the RAF, and I know now he is flying operationally again with Bob Oxspring and 'Cholmondley' Cox from Manston. He will kill himself yet.

The other was Mortimer Rose. F/Lt M Rose, DFC & Bar to be exact, was a ferry pilot at Gibraltar, chafing his cheeks to get into the fighting. So one day he ferried a replacement Spit up to 93 Squadron at Khemis, and refused to go back. He was so persistent that he flew 'Arse-end Charlie' for '93' for about two weeks like a sprog Sergeant pilot. Finally the Group Captain arranged for him to take over a flight in 111 Squadron. The day his official posting to the squadron came through, he was killed. It was he who had collided with Gilroy in the air on the Khemis circuit.

SOUK EL KHEMIS   12-3-43

Things are very quiet just now, I think the calm before a storm. The Middle East Command has kind of incorporated us, and while the change over of organization is taking place there is only defensive readiness. Much has already changed but we have not yet been affected. Originally here, there were four fighter squadrons, 72, 93, III and 152 on the one aerodrome. Now there are three aerodromes and two more fighter squadrons, 242 and 243, and a Beau night-fighter squadron, 600, and two army co-op squadrons, 225 and 241.

This conglomeration of aircraft is to be further increased, so that soon we shall be like XI Group on Dieppe day.

We are still living at the farm, though we shall have to move soon due to the malaria season coming on, and due to our IX's needing a longer runway such as is at Waterloo. We have had the new aircraft over a week now and have had a most interesting time learning about them, especially the engines, and latterly inventing modifications to stop the sand getting into them as they have no air filters like the VB. But those games are not finished yet, so more later.

Also we have had our first crash due to technical failure since we came out here. Tom Hughes had to force land, South of here, over the mountains and near the lines. This was about 5 o'clock in the evening.

I went out to look for him, in case he might be hurt and to find the cause of the crash. I looked for him with Michael McCaul from the orderly room who could read the stars, all that night in the hills, finally getting three hours sleep in an Arab tent fifteen miles away, on the floor. Our Arab hosts, three of them, were very courteous; moreover they knew where the aircraft we were looking for was, and guided us to it in the morning. It only took a few seconds to see that the throttle control had parted for lack of a locking split pin. As we were examining the rest of the aircraft with a view to my deciding whether it could be salvaged or not a Spitfire with Danny Daniels' markings flew over and dropped a message for us which contained good news. It said that we were in friendly territory and that there was a road to it via a town called Teboursouk, also friendly, so Danny was sending a light lorry around from Souk el Khemis right away to pick us up – about

30 miles round the hills. When the van arrived and we were returning via Teboursouk, I noticed that the little town, built on the side of the hills, all white Arab buildings in the sun, was a charming village, untouched by the war. When we got back to Khemis the first person I looked for was, of course, Tom. The Arabs had not known where he was except that he had disappeared back up into the hills in a southerly direction by himself. He had arrived back about half an hour ahead of us, exhausted and delirious and the Doctor had put him to bed. When he saw me, all he said was, "Thank you for looking for me all night Spanner. It was the throttle control wasn't it? So I suppose there was nothing I could have done about it?" I went looking for Sergeant North who had been doing the reconnection job. He somewhat shamefacedly admitted that the coffee truck had come around while he was in the middle of the job and that he must have forgotten to put the split pin back after the interruption. Of such small errors are crashes made. It had taken Tom twenty hours of struggling over the mountains in the dark to get back.

KHEMIS   14-3-43

While in Constantine I visited a brothel for the first time. One afternoon, when there was time to explore, I set out alone following the directions of some members of the Squadron who had already found the Hotel Belvedere. It was on one side of a square in which many Arabs were holding a market so, amidst the crowd of moving, picturesque people, I stood opposite the Hotel, watching for half an hour or so. I saw that men in regular uniform could not get in due to Military Police outside and a large notice inside the door when it opened stated in English that the place was 'Out of Bounds'. I also noticed that, of the Frenchmen who went up to the door, only the well dressed or high ranking ones were allowed in by the big grim doorkeeper. Others and Arabs, soldiers etc. were turned away if they approached. It looked alright but the problem was how to get past the MPs. I waited a while longer until a commotion started round the corner, whistles blowing, people crowding and so on.

The police had all become absent to attend to the commotion down the road, whatever it was, and a smartly dressed, slightly plump, young lady stepped out of the mass of onlookers and made calmly for the Hotel door, walking with a slight roly-poly motion. She was wearing a light beige overcoat, not a spot on it. I managed to catch a glimpse of her face; yes, definitely a nice disposition. By the alacrity with which the front door was smoothly opened and closed to let her in it was obvious that the dragon doorkeeper knew her so I supposed she was one of the regulars coming back from lunch. All in all I liked the look of her so that I made up my mind to follow her and see what happened. The commotion down the road was still going on and the dragon came out of her fastness to have a look, so I became next to her. With a truly French jerk of her head towards the still open front door she said, "Vite Monsieur, vite". So I slipped in. Inside there was a small hall, and I being rather at a loss what to do next, her grimness relaxed a little as she straight way rounded a corner and yelled upstairs "Cocotte!" I was met at the top of the stairs by Cocotte, who was evidently the sales Madame of the place. She was in great spirits and led me along a corridor and into one room, then out again to another further yet, chatting gaily. The place was discreetly furnished, quiet and very clean — like a respectable English hotel; I saw no-one else while she left me to myself in the second room which was perhaps a bedroom but without a bed saying, "Un moment, Monsieur — ssh; les gendarmes". So I sat in an easy chair and waited, rather interested in the security provisions. Evidently my RAF cap badge gave me some precedence in this place for I noticed that I was treated separately and with the greatest of gay decorum. I was pleased with the frankness of it all; there were no questions and no suggestions. I wondered what would happen next.

After a minute or two, Cocotte came back and led me straight to another room wherein I was welcomed by Roly-Poly herself. The French are quite subtle enough to recognize whom I was after without words. Cocotte asked me how long I would like to stay; "Une heure Monsieur, ou une demi-heure?" I said "une demi-heure" would do nicely and bought them both a drink.

Cocotte in due course left Roly-Poly and I to ourselves, discreetly closing the door behind her as she left.

Roly-Poly was great fun and eventually I opened her door and peeped out. There were no intruders to be seen in either direction and so with the best Maurice Chevalian air I could muster I strolled back down the corridor. When I reached the Dragon, she hurriedly waved me behind the door:

"Attendez Monsieur, s'il vous plait" and with a large grin added, "les Polices Militaires" as she pointed outside. I thought, 'how nice of her' and grinned back, doing as I was told. She opened the door and peered outside, then came in and told me to take my cap off and put it under my arm. Trusting her implicitly I did so.

Another peer out . . . Then laughing for once, she made me crouch down, almost on all fours, opened the door and thrust me out.

I saw why when I was loping along outside, well down. There were four or five French soldiers standing in a row outside, protecting me from the view of two MP's behind them. When I got to the end of the line, I stood up, appearing from nowhere, as if I had been there all the time. As I sauntered away through the market I turned and gave the thumbs-up sign to the Doorkeeper who had been checking my welfare all the time. She grinned and replied with the same signal before going back inside her fastness.

SOUK EL KHEMIS   30-3-43

Recently got back from a rush trip to Thelepte servicing the squadron on a day's operations with the USAF. About a month ago the Germans broke through in that locality, took Thelepte aerodromes and advanced towards Tebessa and up the Kasserine gap. They had been stopped by the 6th Armoured Division reinforcing the Yanks from the North, and had since been forced to retire. The trip, although only lasting two days there and back continuously, was most interesting, and adventurous in that we had three mishaps. We arrived back with eight less men and one less lorry than we started off with, but no-one was killed, the lorry is now salvaged running and the pilots shot down two, damaged two more in the one day's flying, without loss. Also the morale effect of our Spit IX's on that front must have been considerable.

After a normal day's flying, one evening, I was called by the CO at about 8 pm from trying to debog a Bedford in the dark, urgent like.[21] "I've got a job for you Spanner. Bags of work, now". He showed me Thelepte on the map, South, and we ran over a road to it, 200 miles. "You have got to be there by tomorrow morning with a servicing party for three days or less. I was pleased as Punch at the chance of some action, and not realising that the Americans were already flying from Thelepte, had visions of great excitement. Tiny was there too, bouncing round with grinning advice. I got cracking on the phone calling the chiefs of the various sections to immediate conference. F/Sgt Landon (B Flight), Sgt Cousins (A Flight), W/O Norton (Armourers), W/O Weedon (Signals), F/Sgt Carver (MT), F/Sgt Daw (i/c here in my absence). We decided to take about 40 men and seven 3-tonners. All to meet outside the cookhouse at 9.30 pm with kit, and board the lorries for loading, up at the aerodrome. Then I had a quick dinner, packed up my bed, borrowed a rifle and drove down to the cookhouse in the jeep. There we got the men, some rubbing sleep out of their eyes as they were routed out of their tents on to the lorries and away to the aerodrome.

Then we loaded two lorries with armament, one with signals, one with flight equipment, one with petrol and oil. Everybody worked like hell, rumours flew round. We were going to join the 8th Army advance. We were going to an aerodrome captured that night. We were going to stop the French being dive-bombed. We were going through enemy territory. The blokes were tumbling over themselves to come. During this activity by the light of torches and headlights, Cpl Jenkins, one of the drivers, fell down a slit trench in the darkness and laid himself out. That was our first mishap. We got the ambulance up, dispatched him to the Doc and I substituted Cpl Peterson (an RAF Service Policeman) who was doing aerodrome guard, who had been our cook-driver on the first Bone to Souk el Arba journey. We were loaded and ready to move off in convoy by about midnight. F/Sgt Landon as usual was with Ginger in the first lorry.

I called all the drivers together and briefed them over a map laid on the ground by torchlight:

"Get these names down, Souk el Arba, Le Kef, Thala, Kasserine, Thelepte which is just here, by Feriana. The kites take off here at 8 am tomorrow so we've got to move fast. First lorry can use headlights, rest only tail lights. After dawn, keep well spread out so you can only just see the man ahead; at least 400 yds and have a spotter on top. Grigg (MT Fitter) is in the jeep with me. He'll attend to breakdowns. No one else to stop. We'll break for a cup of tea when 'Chiefy' Landon stops somewhere past Le Kef. OK? Right. Let's get going."

And the wagons roared away one by one with their load of equipment and men into the night, until all you could see was the train of red tail lights moving, and the red sparks of a thrown out cigarette end hitting the road.

We reached the halt just beyond Le Kef, which was about half way, at about 3.30am with no troubles beyond a few minor adjustments to one or other lorry. 'Big Bill' boiled climbing the winding road through the mountains. Everybody was sleepily cheerful. Cup of tea, sandwich, fill up.

Not long after we started off again one of the lorries pulled up. It was Bill L who, I discovered afterwards, had lost his nerve ever since the Beaufighter bomb landed on top of the wagon in front of him at Arba, and who should never have come on this trip. He said that he couldn't trust himself from going off to sleep – which I had warned the drivers to stop for – and so I put him in the jeep with Grigg and took his 3-tonner myself. It was fully loaded and was great fun driving it with the weight up.

As we moved South the sky got lighter, without hardly noticing it until it dawned that we could see around us. We came through Thala just at dawn, and a more ghostlike, still, deserted village you cannot imagine. We roared one after another up the main street between white houses. Maybe an open window swung on its hinges. No sign of inhabitants, a few destroyed buildings, but mainly a deserted village. We carried on through the Kasserine Pass, and here and there we passed a smashed up lorry, riddle-holed, burnt out, or the tracks of a tank and further on the remains of the tank itself. On one place there was a Churchill tank surrounded by three German tanks, all wrecked, and nearby a little bed of wooden crosses growing in the desert scrub. In another, a cactus grove, there were at least three big Bedfords and an Armoured car all left a wrangling mass of rusting metal, and again the cross bed. They had evidently been caught resting there, from the air, and strafed. Another strange thing — the absence of Arabs. Unusually, there were no Arabs about South of Thala, we saw none throughout the trip. This was because the Arabs in that locality were hostile.

Then came our second mishap. About 7.30, having passed Kasserine and only being about eight miles from Thelepte, Chiefy Landon stopped the first wagon for a breather, being ahead of schedule. The others pulled up behind, except me and two others, who having been delayed, were well behind. The blokes got out to stretch their legs, the drivers began to check their fuel and oil. There was a dead donkey off the side of the road, which attracted the curiosity of several of the men. While they were standing round this, looking at and kicking it, an explosion went off and five or six of them collapsed to the ground. Everyone else threw themselves down onto the ground, instinctively thinking they were being bombed. But there was no aircraft noise. Landon came to his senses first. It was a landmine, left from the German retreat. He told Sgt. Cousins to go back to the Red Cross people of Kasserine for help, reviewed the situation, got the people that had been hit wrapped up in blankets against shock. AC Hitt had a piece of shrapnel in his foreleg which had evidently cut a main artery for he was fast losing blood. With the help of an armourer AC Foot, who kept his head and 'knew how' from his London ARP days, he applied a tourniquet tight around the thigh and succeeded in stopping the blood. The American Red Cross people arrived but they could do little but make the wounded as comfortable as possible and gave them some pills. About then I came up to the back lorry and hearing that "someone's hit a land mine ahead" and seeing the alarmed faces, I drove as fast as I could up the road, wondering when I was going to hit a mine in the sand. I came up to the scene, shook hands with an American doctor who said "There's a pretty bad surgical case here, must get him to the field operating theatre at Feriana quickly". Chiefy Landon said five were seriously hurt, and he thought Hitt and Cpl Fowler, who had been hit in the back and could not breath properly, were pretty bad. I saw Hitt's grey colour and thought he'd had it, and told Cpl Fowler this was pretty serious and we were going to rush them to hospital. I ordered Sgt. Cousins to proceed with all the other men to the aerodrome at once. Then with one man, who had shrapnel in his arm, drove off like mad to get ambulances and surgeons from Feriana.

I found the emergency surgical unit and was shown straight in to the OC without ado. He immediately ordered out two ambulances, and told me to bring the RAF boys in here as fast as I could. While leading the ambulances back, I saw "kites" flying overhead in formation, and so, telling the ambulances the way, left them and made for the aerodrome which I could see from the road. As the CO touched down I came across the field to meet him and we sorted out a dispersal which he taxied over to. As the rest of the pilots came in, the lorries of my men drove up. The first kite was re-fuelled by a Motor Mechanic and a Despatch Rider but we made it. That was the second time, after a long journey, I have met Bob Oxspring coincidentally, air to ground (the other time was at the Dieppe show).

When things had settled down a bit I drove off again in the jeep to see how Chiefy Landon and the ambulances were getting on. I met him a few miles away coming down the road in his 3-tonner with the remainder of the crews. He told me that the ambulances had got the men away efficiently. Next day, when we had time, the senior NCO's and I went back to visit them in the hospital. We found that four of them; all except Hitt, had been moved that day into Tebessa. The field hospital only could keep those who could not be moved. The American doctor was very decent and said that they had given Hitt two blood transfusions; and so through the quickness in rendering the right First Aid by F/Sgt. Landon and the efficiency of the American surgery, Hitt's life, at least was saved. We were allowed to go and see Hitt and found him in a ward of men gravely wounded. On either side was a close row of beds and in them men in all conditions, with limbs, hands, even faces missing – or hanging from the ceiling in bandages.

There was a queer smell, of chemicals I suppose, and around the beds there moved American nurses, Women! – in smart uniforms, who gave hope and cheerfulness to the place. Up and down the middle walked a doctor who when he saw us around Hitt's bed, exclaimed "You can't kill an Englishman" and then repeated it.

When Landon and I returned to the aerodrome, the pilots were about to take off on a sweep. We saw them off, and set about making some sort of temporary camp. All the kites got back; and the pilots, and the Americans when they heard, were very excited for they had shot down at least two Huns. Tired out though we were by this time, this news kept us going the rest of the day and made us feel the whole effort was worth while. There was one more sweep that day, from which the squadron flew straight home.

That evening I got orders from Ops. to return to Khemis at once. This I disregarded for we had been going 36 hours non-stop already. We slept twelve hours, some in tents, others in the backs of lorries, and what a marvellous sleep it was.

Next morning, after visiting Hitt in hospital and giving orders to be ready to move off after lunch, I spent with the American Group Engineer for whom I had promised I would re-set the engine controls of their slowest Spit. Which I did, instructing several of their very fine technical men in the Merlin controls which are so important and which though locked out of adjustment frequently, are not taught by the RAF text books. The aircraft, on test, then out-climbed the fasted kite they had, and I scrounged a 6 ft steel rule for the job. Also I showed him our home-made jettisonable air filter, which was demonstrated, and which he took drawings of, agreeing that although rather Heath Robinson like, it worked, and was the best we could do against sand in the field. Then at lunch I confirmed with Ops. that there were no further orders for us, and so prepared to leave.

The lads enjoyed themselves greatly at Thelepte. It was an aerodrome set almost in the desert and you could not see across it for a rise in the middle. The food was marvellous, varied, rich, sweet — for instance, peanut butter, honey, sweet corn, fruit juices to drink. The RAF seems to have a good name with the Americans, especially these front line ones, many of whom had been on English stations. We were treated like Lords, and with the American easy hospitality. The blokes loved it and shot huge lines with their Yankee 'oppos'. We were sorry to leave and since then many of them have asked me if there is any chance of going back.

On the way back Landon and I went ahead in the Jeep to look for Cpl Fowler and Co. who were supposed to be near Tebessa. It is a walled Arab town with about three empty French shops in it, set between mountain ranges on desert scrub. Outside the walls, which encircle the old garrison town are built in odd places the usual French municipal buildings; Post Office, Gendarmerie, etc. Fowler's bunch had been flown back to Algiers.

The main convoy got ahead of us there, and we did not catch them up until well north of Thala again, just about dusk where we all stopped for supper in a cactus grove. On the way we drove over miles of lonely road through barren hills. Desolate. At one place, on the Tunisian frontier, there were some Roman ruins, the first I have ever seen. A theatre, and arch, and many pillars and old corner stones. I wondered what the town could have been like then, for now it was miles from nowhere, desert scrub, and high in the rolling hills.

After supper we started off again into the darkness. Lorry after lorry. I was driving a 3-tonner again, because I liked it. There was nothing to report until, coming down the steep road the other side of Le Kef into the Souk el Arba plain there occurred our third mishap. Cpl Spink, driving a 3-tonner full of men went over the side on a bend, and turned his wagon over. When I came along the headlights revealed the gruesome sight of one of our 'Thorney's' on its side in a dip beside the road. But no-one was hurt, the men were transferred to other lorries, Spink and a volunteer were left to guard the wagon (which was salvaged and brought in next day) and we drove on and on through the darkness, past Souk el Arba, up the familiar Messerschmidt alley and pulled in to our Khemis farm about two o'clock in the morning.

Since my last entry a brief history. From that date until Tunis was taken by the 1st Army, the flying never ceased. We stayed on our aerodrome at Khemis, and the "only a few more days' effort" went on and on. Three and four sweeps per day. Last month, April, we did 898 flying hours. The serviceability only went under 12-up once, and that was ten.

The armourers created an RAF record of only 1:1,800 stoppages with belt feed ammunition, and the squadron score went up and up, ending the campaign at 52, top score. III Squadron were next with 50, and 81 Squadron third. Against our 52 Huns we had only five pilots killed by enemy action, and the number of Spitfires we had used was 77.

I had flown down to Algiers, stopping on the way to spend a day with 'Roly Poly' at Constantine, when I read in the papers that Tunis had fallen. I had not thought that would happen, having lost hope of the Army breaking through for some months after all. Algiers were to arrange about engine changes for Spit IX's and try and get some gen on engine cutting. I got back as fast as I could in time to move with the squadron to here, La Sebala, about ten miles North of Tunis near the sea, on the 12th. Since being here the flying has slackened off to a negligible amount of readiness and we have been spending our time resting, reorganizing, and scrounging German and Italian equipment, and bathing in the sea.

The story of the famous Farish phantom filter.

When we were re-equipped, in February I think, with the Spit IX's, they came without any type of air filter or cleaner on them. The Spit V's we have out here all have a Vokes Air Cleaner permanently over the engine air intake fixed integrally with the belly cowling, this to stop sand and dust.

One day, shortly after getting the IX's, Pete Fowler went over to Bone to 81 Squadron for the only engine hand-book (of which the Orderly Room typed out three copies in two days) and any other gen he could pick up. When he came back he told me that '81' were trying to design an air filter for IX's, having already produced two which were no good.

This set me thinking. There were two premises. First that any filter placed permanently over the air intake would affect the performance at altitude, even though as large as that on the 'V' which we couldn't make anyway. Secondly that any type of filter must be simple, and so possible to make in the field. The best idea appeared to be a flapped filter, to allow either filtered air or direct air intake according to the position of the legs, as in the 'Lightning', or at the pilot's control as in the German design. (This was designed, and one produced after a month or two, by Harris of '81'). But it did not seem practical to me to make for all our aircraft in the field quickly. I wanted something simpler but which would do until base Algiers modified all kites to the flapped clamshell (Messerschmidt) filter which I thought they would have to work on and which would probably take them several months to perfect and produce.

So what meanwhile?

There came the idea of a jettisonable air filter, fixed over the air intake, and pulled off by the undercarriage retraction. Sgt. Gilbert and I designed one on those lines, with a catch at the top, attached to the starboard leg, by a piece of steel wire, and a deflector plate on the bottom to overcome by wind resistance the air intake suction, after the release when it came down on a small parachute. The echelon made this and Pete Fowler tried it out in the air. We got the filter to drop alright after changing the size of the deflection plate once or twice, but after it had been dropped four or five times, from varying altitudes and never got bent much, and we couldn't get the parachute to open properly, we discarded the idea of the parachute. Pete Fowler was very good, patiently doing circuits and bumps in the air tests.

It seemed practical. All the pilots were flat out for it. The Group Captain told the CO that a great deal depended on it in the coming air battle. The echelon got cracking and fitted all the kites up, one by one — except one, 'H' never got done — and kept repairing and replacing them as they got bent. This went on for about six weeks, and kept four of my most skilled fitters permanently employed. They did a damn good job. Meanwhile the flying got more and more. It was a fine sight at dispersal when the squadron took off, and twelve kites used to fly over, one after the other dropping their filters in all directions. (By this time the thing had been considerably improved with modifications, one per day I had ideas, including the use of the Plessey gun control for releasing it from the cockpit, and a contact light to tell the pilot when it had fallen off.) Many people used to watch it.

The Group Engineers, of whom Harris, ex 81 Squadron was now one, were aware of these goings on. The amount of flying became hectic as the air fighting grew more intense day after day. We maintained our 12-up serviceability though. And 81 Squadron maintenance cracked up. 'Ops' screamed to Group; Group, who had already begun to doubt the practical effectiveness of it, decided without consulting me, that it was our air filter that was making the difference . . . It was not actually . . . just luck and better maintenance. 81 Squadron were ordered to adopt our filter at once which pleased me somewhat.

I had been getting 110 Repair and Salvage Unit to mass produce the filters for us by this time. Now 110 RSU and SU moved away to service the Yanks. Also 'H' had never had a filter fitted and, after 80 hours, still caused no more trouble than the others. Full engine life in those days was about 100 hours only. Also the filters were getting bent and lost, so that the flight men spent hours looking for them. Also we were flying like hell with no sign of relief, and I couldn't spare the men. Also they sometimes wouldn't release and it was always the leader of the show who had to come back, it seemed. But 'H' decided me: we stopped using the filters.

We made a hand filter instead, simply a cover to be put over the air intake at all times when it was on the ground, including running up, and removed by an airman's hand just before the pilot signalled 'take off'. Then replaced by hand at the end of each landing run, before taxi-ing away.

That was the end of the jettison air-filter as far as I was concerned but the famous phantom filter wasn't so easy to kill.

We had given Group, and 81, a prototype of the flapped filter. 81 fitted it on their CO's kite and used it for a period during which they got little trouble from this one, and bags from the others. The reason for this was because the CO always took off first and so did not meet the chief cause of sand in engines, that due to the wake of the previous aircraft on strips, where they screamed for filters to be made. But 81 Squadron did not realize this. They must take off one by one. Group found the Repair and Salvage Units could not do it and that they would have to get higher authority to get 144 Maintenance Unit at Algiers to do it.

So the Chief Mechanical Staff Officer, Middle East Command – Air Vice Marshal Dawson, came down to the IX Squadrons to investigate the matter for himself. He came to us in a tearing hurry. Group knew that we had stopped using the filters after full experience, except for the hand type, but '81' had kicked up a fuss that they were necessary, and so I don't think Dawson was told that. He asked us what troubles we were having etc., took a boost control unit to pieces himself, asked Sgt. North how often he had to clean the sand out of them, and buggered off with a fairly correct impression that the sand problem was nothing to worry about really. But, 81 Squadron kept him the rest of the afternoon and with Group's help, persuaded him to adopt 'their' filter.

Harris told me later that the Air Vice Marshal had approved of the thing, whereas I told Harris it was no good. Being very busy with the last phase of the campaign (three and four sweeps per day) I heard nothing more until I was in Algiers at North West African Air Service Command. There, talking to the technical staff officers, the Wing Commanders and Squadron Leaders who push out all the bumph, and were especially interested to hear about the operation of Merlin 61 engines in the field, and were interesting to hear on high theory and policy, the question came up as to what troubles we were having. After a long discussion on the case of engines cutting in a dive, during which I learnt a lot, I mentioned boost surge due to sand sticking up the boost control, as a nuisance. They all jumped on me.

"Oh, you needn't worry about that any more, Farish old boy, we've got the answer to all sand troubles, a tropical modification of all Spitfire IX's, here's the leaflet, this will stop all the sand and it doesn't affect the performance at altitude like the Vokes, we're making them for you as fast as we can — here is a model." And they produced my jettisonable filter!

Luckily the campaign came to an end the next day.

EXTRACT FROM A LETTER TO MOTHER 3-6-43 [22]

" . . . Now at Mateur, I have developed the art of comfort in campaigning to a fine skill, and compared with our original ignorant wretchedness in the mud of Souk el Arba, it is worth describing. So here is a typical day. Mind you we were off operations, i.e. resting.

Wake up in the morning about nine o'clock and, donning a pair of shorts and a shirt, descend from my still blacked out caravan into the bright sunlight for breakfast in the open air. Then a comfortable bowel exercise on a real round seat placed with a view and to leeward of my caravan. Then, for the rest of the morning while 'Fletch', my clerk, guard,

A SONG TO THE TUNE OF "BLUES IN THE NIGHT" SUNG BY THE AIRMEN DURING THESE TIMES

From Khemis to Medjez, from Medjez to Tunis
From Tunis to Pont du Fahs.
I've seen me some light flak, I've been on some Tac R's

But there is one thing I know
A trench is a safe place, when 88s do and 190s too
Are bombing Waterloo.

Now the warnings calling, now the bombs are falling
Woo-ho! Controller done told me,
'Treble one scramble' to 25 grand and put up a stand
Oh 'Negum', knock 'em down.

From Souk el Arba to Pichon from Pichon to Thala
From Thala to Kasserine, I've escorted 'Hurries' and one or
two big boys.

But there is one thing I know, etc...

— — — — —

Glossary:

Flak	Anti-aircraft fire.
Tac R	Tactical Air Reconnaissance.
88	Junkers JU88.
190	Focke-Wulf 190.
Treble one	III Squadron, who were on 'Waterloo', one of the Khemis runways, the longest, which 72 Sqadron used.
25 grand	altitude 25,000 feet.
Negum	III Squdron call-sign over RT (radio transmission)

servant, cook and messenger, sweeps out the home, I drive round the flights in my jeep supervising work on the grounded kites, and the overhaul of our ground equipment and Mechanical Transport. Maybe call on another Engineer Officer for a cup of tea and a gossip on the other side of the 'drome about 11 am. Then a light lunch in the heat of the day.

We do no work in the afternoon, so I collect any pilots who are so inclined and together we drive off to Ferryville, beside the blue lake where we swim and sunbathe all afternoon. There are spring boards, high boards, a water polo pitch, and there we meet many people we know from other squadrons and from our own. Back to the aerodrome for tea, and then if necessary a little gentle work from five to seven-thirty in the cool of the evening.

What shall we do tonight? Go to the flea-pit cinema in Mateur, or go dancing at our friend Madame B...'s house with their two beautiful daughters. — One, the younger, has jet black hair in waves, a pair of sparkling eyes set in a pretty face, and a tan skin which her all-white frock offsets as it clings to her lithe figure. And can she dance? She is made for it, as her red lips part and her white eyes flash in the dark face when she sways in the tango. (She's aged 14!) Or perhaps we go to the films held on the side of a hill with the screen set at the bottom and many soldiers, thousands, lying, sitting or standing round on the grass or on lorries. It is a warm night, and you can see and hear perfectly in the open. And when the show is finished, if you are quick away, you can look back and see a scene that tears your heart for peace, that of many headlights of lorries and cars streaming out. The whole field is lit up, the sand dust catches the light and holds it, and one after another the bright headlights come towards you in a long line. It reminds one of Hyde Park on New Year's eve.

Then home, drive up to the caravan and connect up to the wandering lead, for the lighting of it, to the car battery, and so after a quiet read from my library, to bed . . . . "

RAF HALFAR, MALTA   12-6-43

From La Sebala we moved to Mateur for a short two weeks or so of re-equipping. On 5th June 1943, after loading all our equipment on thirteen 3-ton lorries — the complete mobile squadron — we set off in convoy for Sfax, about 200 miles South on the coast. We were going overseas again. The Wing HQ and five squadrons all drove down that day, each in convoy.

We pulled in and made camp about ten miles outside Sfax at a quarter past seven in the evening of the morning on which we had started out. We were the only squadron to make it in one day — the rest and Wing, rolled in all the next day — and also we were complete with every lorry when we halted. This success was in no small way due to the 'Thorneys' we had, as a result of a great argument, bluffing and sheer disobedience. The day before we left, Group produced about fifty new 3-ton Bedfords to be distributed to squadrons. 'Thorneys' are so much better than Bedfords, that I would not let our 'Thorneys' go. Nor would "Judy" Garland, Engineer Officer for Wing. All the other squadrons were re-equipped with Bedfords. I had a fight all that day, had to order Supply and Transport men off our lorries, etc. and played every trick I knew for I was sure our old Thorneys, even after six month's campaigning, were better than Bedfords. Judy and I won in the end.

The country on the journey was interesting. South of Tunis it was rolling hills, with light sandy earth and many stumpy trees, until we reached Enfidaville. From there we deluged onto a flat plain, just sand and olive groves in the sand. As we move South it seemed to grow hotter! You could see what the Western Desert must have been like. Just endless sand, with some olive trees grouped here and there and through the middle the straight metal shining hot road, ever on. We passed through the outskirts of Sousse and also later Sfax, and again the architecture was different from that of North Africa. Much less European buildings — those that were, of a special sort of anti-heat design, rather nice — but mostly the peaked oriental arch and mosaics and flat roofs.

We stayed about two days outside Sfax camping with light packs only in the sand. I had brought my caravan which was very useful. On the third day we embarked all our vehicles on the ships. I had to leave my ex-German caravan behind.

The ship was a tank landing craft American built, all welded. It is best described by taking a tanker, and putting vehicles instead of oil, inside and on top of the tank. Access was gained to the ship through the bows. Two great doors swung outwards, and then a ramp or drawbridge came down, over which the lorries were driven into the gaping hold. There, the heavies stayed below while the lighter wagons went up on a lift to the open deck. All vehicles were backed in. They were then shackled, back and front axles, to the steel floor by chains and turn buckles. At the stern was the engine room, office and crew's quarters; along each side there were bunks for the troops, and along the bottom there were air ballast tanks. This was to give increased buoyancy for landing on beaches; thus, with her flat bottom and ballast tanks blown up, the ship drew only four feet at the bows and seventeen feet at the stern. Normally the ballast tanks were not inflated, although on the way over, at sea, some were blown up to raise the ship over any torpedoes that may have been about. The engines were two V-12 2-stroke Diesels developing about 1,400 HP each. Speed 11 knots. On each ship was carried two complete squadrons of about 50 large vehicles and 400 men. Easily.

These ships were ideal for the job. The next day we embarked and pushed off for a very comfortable 26 hour journey. I slept on deck. We sighted Malta that morning but didn't pull into the Grand Harbour at Valetta until noon.

That place, the Grand Harbour is worth remarking on. You come in the entrance in a fairly big ship and you are just surrounded by houses, tiers of them, with people waving out of the windows. It is a marvellous harbour, being long and with deep creeks in which two or three warships may be laying. Obviously the war has been there. Many gaps in the rows of houses, piles of rubble, and a number of astonishing bits of rusty ships sticking up out of the water in all directions. But stone, warm stone, is the predominating feature. It is a sort of soft brown stone, all the houses, monuments public buildings, bridges are built of it, and above the town the country stretches away over the hills in a series of brown stone walls.

We poured off the ship, a stream of roaring heavy lorries, and drove with many people waving to us and watching the scruffily clothed, tanned men in the darkly camouflaged wagons and trailers, through Valetta by winding roads to RAF station Hal Far.

This place Malta, and Hal Far in particular, is bloody awful as far as work goes. It stinks of bullshit. There is bumph, forms, reports, returns, regulations galore.[23] No transport to speak of. The natives are loath to part with the glory of seige conditions and never cease reminding us of the island's shortages — which no longer exist.

To illustrate this, there was an incident the moment we arrived. 'B' flight lorries had no sooner pulled into a 'pen' on the side of the 'drome than, a wait for pitching orders being apparent, two dirty airmen decided to brew up. Tin can out of the back of the wagon. Put some sandy earth in it, poured petrol well in to saturate and lit up. Normal procedure in the desert but along comes one of the 'island' station masters and seeing the char (tea), tears a terrific strip off the astonished airmen. "Wasting petrol. Don't you realize that every drop of that stuff has cost men lives to get it through to the island? etc. etc." To us petrol was less indispensable than water, quite apart from 9,000 gallons a day we used running engines.

I hate it all and wish to be back in the field quickly. There are sheets to sleep in though, and a little better food, and cinemas to which I go pretty well every night.

Of Malta and my doings here during last month. Since the North African victory there has been little air activity in the Mediterranean area from either side, with perhaps the exception of the Allied bombers over Pantelleria and now Sicily. This had affected us, in '72' in that although there always seems something that ought to be done, yet we find time slow. There is no absorption in work, it's a sort of half existence, half work, one sweep or so a day, half civilisation again, cinemas, sailing, beer, women, yet none of it — except for me the sailing with Tom Hughes, worthwhile. The cinemas are too hot and the sound is often inaudible. The beer is grand, when there is any, which is about one night a week. The women speak English with a Maltese accent which I don't like, and have known uniforms too long. Unlike the French, they have no style; they are a cross between the Paramount dance-hall Jewesses of London and the Arabs of North Africa.

To describe the island. The most remarkable thing about it is the smallness of it. Small houses, small fields, And from almost any point you can see the sea. It is a contrast to French North Africa. There is no such thing as a straight road, they are mostly very narrow, tarmac, and with the inevitable stone wall high on either side. Besides the smallness there is the stone. From the ship coming in, it looked a barren place, all of light coloured yellow-brown stone. That was about right. Sandstone. The many buildings of all shapes and sizes are built all of this sandstone. Every road is hedged with it. The diminutive fields are walled with it and it sticks up through the ground and all along the sea shore. So that, when the sun is full out, as it is now, the place is bright.

"I have sat by the Mediterranean sea, with my eyes clenched against the brightness of sandstone cliffs, of sparkling water, of Latine rigged sails, and I have wished she were with me.

I have driven a heavily laden wagon over wet high winding roads and over dry sandy desert roads, endlessly, and pulling in at nightfall to make camp I have wished she were with me.

I have looked across wide aerodromes in the evening, across sand, muddy rivers, towards the Atlas mountains and I have wished she were with me."

The buildings are a queer architecture. There are the rows of square sandstone dwelling houses with every one of them a balcony of wood — the Maltese balcony — sticking out from the middle of the first floor window. There are many magnificent churches and cathedrals. Every three or four houses have a church; two I remark on in particular. One is on a rise, a big round cathedral thing, huge dome supported on arches all the way round. Roman. The other is a very beautiful Gothic church, on the side of a hill near Hamrun. It has a tall spire and is set among cypress trees, some of the few trees on the island. The streets of the town are very narrow.

Finally there are the people. The Maltese, dark skinned, crossed between Italy and Africa. And the enormous British garrison. Navy, Army, Air Force everywhere. Of course there are no Americans and no French which is a contrast to Tunisia. The island is over-populated and the Maltese wax lazily prosperous swindling and civil-serving the British.

Of sailing I would describe a 16 ft Sharpe Bermuda rigged dinghy. It has red sails and heavy, slow tiller and in it every day Tom and I sail about Pretty Bay among small naval ships, tankers, a merchant-man wrecked, other small sailing boats, Maltese rowing boats plying their Black Market trade with ships, and clear blue water.

An amusing incident occurred with one of the low stone walls in Malta which I have mentioned as being all over the place. I forgot to enter the story in my diary at the time but can insert it appropriately here. One moonlit night I was returning from one of the Messes to Hal Far on my motorbike at a good clip because I had had a little bit to drink. Came to one of those right-angle turns in the road which I didn't see in the moonlight so I drove straight on into one of those low stone walls. Both my bike and myself went over the top of the wall and the bike was still running though slightly bent. I switched it off and waited for rescue which wasn't too long in coming. Had to take a couple of days off in hospital but was really only bruised.

I have to explain some air force jargon for you to understand the joke which was made at a concert which was held in the field shortly afterwards. A "Spinner" is the small cowling which is mounted on most aircraft in front of the propellor to smooth the air-flow around the roots of the propellor; a "kite" is RAF slang for an aeroplane; "Spanner" was my nickname on 324 Wing.

Now, two of our humourists among the airmen had painted their faces black and by arrangement with the producer climbed up onto the stage.

"Did you ever see a spinner fall off a kite?" asks Amos.

Slight pause while Andy considers the question then slowly replies, "No, I don't believe I ever have, but I have seen a "Spanner" fall off a bike."

Roars of laughter from the assembled ranks at my expense.

COMISO SICILY

Of our journey from Malta to here.

On D+3 after the original assault — I forgot the actual date; about a fortnight ago — I left Malta with an advance party of eighteen men of the squadron to join the Commandoes in Sicily. Our kites had not yet moved off, but for the previous four or five days there had been intensive flying from Malta. The most intensive yet — four sweeps a day with jettisonable tanks every time, regularly. That is an average of eight hours multiplied by twelve aircraft = 96 hours a day for four days. And intensive air fighting too. On the third day we broke the island record, knocking thirteen down. We were the top scoring squadron of those in Malta, 21 in all, and shot down 28 during our six weeks stay for the loss of three pilots.

Well, as I was saying, early one morning me and my trusty band moved off to the docks at Sliema. There we were joined by representatives of the other squadrons, making a party of 90 in all, of which, being the only officer present, I was in charge. About 10 am we embarked on a Landing Craft Infantrymen! This was a high speed barge American built, suitable for landing troops on beaches. It could carry 400 fully laden, but we were the only 90 on board. Outside it looked an awful contraption all rust and broken gang-planks. Inside everything was clean and white, cook's galley with refrigerator and two coffee percolators, bunks on the mess decks for everybody. The crew was very small, two young RNVR Lieutenants who were great pals, and about ten men. Together this lot had left New York fresh and inexperienced with the new ship, six weeks before and they had not stopped ever since. They had crossed the Atlantic alone.

I had a great time on the voyage of eight hours. It was grand sitting on the little bridge with the pair of them, splashing through the Med. in the sun, drinking tea and iced drinks alternately, and all the time conversing gaily and interestingly of our respective services. I had a marvellous lunch in their tiny ward room furnished and curtained like a home they had made themselves. I talked with the first mate during his lunch and then over my coffee with the Captain over his, and it was amusing to hear how exactly similar their views and interests were, and how they spoke always of the other, telling their tales of experience. Our topics over that meal ranged over: I remember New York; American women; stocking the ship with supplies galore at the Government's expense; Leagrave and Miss Impey; Landing Craft Infantry-men, Landing Craft Tanks, Motor Torpedo Boats; aeroplanes of all sorts; bullshit and the lack of it; Christmas in North Africa and in New York; the untrainedness and youth of the crew, etc.; and of course, stories from each of them of their previous voyage to Sicily three days before, which was on the assault. They showed me their log on this subject and here is a copy of it:

10.40	Shipped from Malta – Binghi Bay
17.40	Engine manifold on fire. Cut engine out.
18.07	Engine in. Revs 600. Great difficulty in regaining position in convoy.
19.00	Port ramp shifted. Had to reduce to two thirds to secure.
19.20	After winch out of order.
20.00	Speed flank to catch convoy. Pounding. Sea rough. Wind force 12 (high).
00.30	Rejoined convoy. Made many signals about whereabouts of Tegelburg.
02.45	Directed Tegelburg by L/SI North two miles off port bow.
03.30	Came up with 'Senior Naval Office Landing'. Redirected to T.
04.15	Redirected to S.N.O.L. Ordered to stand by.
05.00	Alongside S.N.O.L., embarked troops.
06.00	Beached LCP's and LCI's crossed my beaching course causing bad beaching. Disembarked troops under shell fire. Beach very shallow no kedge.
07.00	Withdrew from beach. Ramps brought in with great difficulty.
09.45	Reported to S.N.O.L.
14.30	Tied alongside Landing Craft Infantry 312.
16.00	Air attack. Dive bombing. Claim hits on plane seen to crash in hill.
16.30	Cast off 312. Made out to sea. Attacked Fw 190 but just out of range. Several attempts to return in-shore but bombing continued.
18.00	Rejoined 12 Flotilla and sailed for Malta.

We sighted Sicily all too soon and having cruised along the coast Eastwards for an hour or two looking for our appropriate beach, which the skipper had not been to before, we eventually beached at Scoglitto, a little fishing village. We waded ashore. (Beaching consists of the boat driving full speed, with all ballast tanks pumped up, as far as it can up the shore and then, having disembarked the troops, pulling itself off again by means of a kedge, or stern anchor, which had previously been dropped on the approach and the cable paid out. Quite an exciting procedure with a large boat.)

On shore, we were confronted with one 3-ton lorry and fifteen miles to move five lorry loads over a bad road. It was about six o'clock in the evening. The wagon made three trips carrying the kit and equipment, and the rest of us — all 90 — set off marching. We hitch-hiked it. Every lorry that came up I stopped, put as many men as possible on board and myself always being the last, yet got lifts most of the way. It is the first time I have hitch-hiked a party of ninety!

Vittoria was the only town through which we had to pass and it so happened that a party of about 30 of us got dropped and so had to march through it. We came through just at dusk, in fine style, singing and making enough noise for a battalion. It was most amusing.

The whole lot were at Comiso aerodrome by about 10 pm, and we just lay down anywhere, crunching biscuits, and slept till dawn.

On the last day of July we moved from Comiso to here. The reason was that Comiso aerodrome was too good for us, having a 2,000 yard runway, camp and being in pleasant surroundings. So in true Air Force fashion the "Staff" moved us to where there is plenty of dust for taxiing — namely Pachino. I have been about the island quite a bit now — of more later — and from Vittoria in the SW to Catania in the North there is no place like this, in our territory, for small winged animals. As one of our airmen put in a letter I was censoring, "All day the flies take off and land on you, and at night its mosquitoes with their ground crews of ants". However, "per ardua ad f.a." (*sic!*)

Comiso lies in a sort of flat valley at the foot of a ridge of hills. There is much fruit all about so that you can reach out your hand and pick a bunch of grapes, or lemons, or peaches as you like. Over this ridge lies a town by the name of Ragusa which is untouched by the war and most "Sicilianly" picturesque. It is built around the junction of two gorges and consists of an old town and a new town. The new town has straight streets criss-crossing, a cathedral and below, a square where the male populace meets in the evenings, and there are many shops, still stocked. The shops have no windows for display but just a large doorway, usually hung with metal string curtain. With its gorge down both sides and its whole society out for a stroll after siesta time in the late afternoon, it is a pleasantly clean and joyful sight, reminding me a little of Constantine, though not so interesting.

Of our doings at Comiso, it was a most singularly dull invasion. I was expecting something like Souk el Arba. I didn't see one single enemy aircraft nor hear one bomb go off. There was little flying. We seemed to have won the air battle from Malta, and after those hectic and all-out four or five days we had air superiority over Sicily completely. The only things of any moment at Comiso in the flying line were Me 109's left in various states of unserviceability as usual, and from these we selected one which had evidently just had a prop change. With the help of Tom Hughes, a German dictionary, and various experiments, a few of our pilots flew it, the CO and Tom mostly, and when we moved to Pachino we brought it with us. Then one evening "the Sexton", now F/O Gear DFC, took off in it, without letting the ack-ack know he was going to fly it and without a Spitfire escort. All the guns for miles around opened up at this Me 109. We were in mental agony lying on our bellies with shrapnel pattering down. A Spit took off in the middle of it all, flew into the gunfire and by circling "Sex", stopped the gunfire, but Sex was so shaken that he came in to land with only one leg down and pranged it on the runway. Much to the OC RA's consternation there was not one bullet hole in it.

But, more important than 109's or Spitfires or any other type of war plane, there was found near Comiso a Caproni moth; dual control; Bi-plane, wood and fabric; six cylinder, in-line, air-cooled, Alfa Romeo engine. The whole pretty well brand new and fully serviceable. The echelon call it the "Maggie", the pilots and I call it the "Pisser"; it is a lovely aeroplane. Faster than a Tiger moth and safer than a Maggie. We have had to modify the tail wheel forks to take a Spit tyre

— which I suppose is the first of a long list of conversions, for we can get no spares for it of course. And we painted 'RN' proudly on the side and for a week or two we flew it like hell. I was up in it most every day. At last the squadron had a Maggie again. It was recognized as an extremely useful, and to me precious, acquisition, what I have always missed in squadrons overseas.

Then one day it had its first prang. Roy Hussey and Scottie, two pilots, took it over to Lentini across country to try and find Griff's grave. During the trip they got shot at by ack-ack fire and saw the 'orrid sight of two Me 109's pass them about 500 yards away. However, when they came back, Scottie, who had never flown it before, was in the front cockpit and, finding the cross-wind a bit awkward at Comiso, asked Roy to try and bring her in. This Roy did in typical fighter pilot fashion, touched down fast right across the runway, not even choosing to run on a grass taxi track, found himself driving straight for a bomb hole and a pile of rubble, reached for the brakes and found they were in the front cockpit. Scottie, sitting there quite obliviously until they hit something, broke the undercarriage and collapsed undignifiedly on the ground.

It took us about a month, with wood, Dural, steel and welding to mend that undercarriage and it is only just ready again now. When we moved the 60 miles or so from Comiso to Pachino we brought 'The Pisser' up on the back of 3-tonners.

About the middle of last month I went from the squadron, at Pachino, on a three day scrounging expedition; Pachino, Noto, Syracuse, Lentini, Catania, Acireale, and back via Augusta. I was scrounging officially for a twenty ton press with which to exchange sleeves in Thorneycroft cylinder blocks; no easy thing to find, and unofficially, for the piano which I had been trying to get for the airmen's mess for six months now, ever since Cpl Brown suggested it at Souk el Khemis; and also for a look around Sicily. It was a most successful trip. We got wind of a press (which eventually materialized some weeks later and did the job), we got a piano at last; a great victory, for so many other blokes had already tried from the squadron; I had been sending lorries out for months looking for one. We saw plenty, and got mixed up in one or two little incidents, including the front line by mistake, a blitz on Augusta, some looting, and the accidental picking up of two most entertaining "hitch hikers". The members of the party, made up as usual on the spur of the moment were F/Sgt. Mann, Sgt. North, W/O Weedon, W/O Norton, all on my invitation for things were quiet, and D/O Fergus King, F/O Roy Hussey, F/Sgt. Morris, an Aussie; and Sgt. Scott also an Aussie, all pilots.

We took Rita, one of my beloved 'Thorneys' and having loaded up with rations, water, blankets, 'mossie' nets, etc. etc., set off one fine morning, with that intoxication which freedom gives at the beginning of a holiday. I was making for the Catania area, knowing there must be REME somewhere near the Army. It was a good road all the way to Syracuse, where we stopped for half an hour to have a look round that romantically named plad it dull, not much damaged, working overtime as a temporary port, and so we left again. We drove North on the Catania road which grew worse as we went along, both for reasons of topography and from enemy demolitions, and from the huge traffic. We passed prisoners of war working, trying to widen the road in the sun and dust.

We made a detour at Melilli, looking for Sgt. Griffith's grave, for Roy. There we climbed high from the coast up the side of a mountain among orchards and terraced vineyards until we came to the village set on the side of the hill, white houses among all the green bright little trees and overlooking the plain and the sea. We stopped there to inquire and looked in at a small shop for fun. I liked the typical houses, with their white or pink walls, serrated roofs and the windows and doors massively set in embossed stone. There were no soldiers about, which was a relief and the people were curious and friendly. We discovered that the graveyard was further on the main coast road and therefore descended to it by a series of rough hair-pin bends. My arms ached by the time we got down, but not for the last time. We found Griff's grave in a row of about ten little mounds of soldier's graves. There was the rough wooden cross; lop-sided with on it written: "Sgt. Griffiths, RAF. Died in air collision." We added "72 Squadron" and "Killed in action" and "Pilot" in ink (the rest was written in pencil) and took some photographs. I promised Roy I would get a decent cross made out of prop. blades.

Then we went on. The road wound into hillier country, with here and there, where 'Jerry' had done a good job, downright cross-country stuff. Four wheel drive and down to bottom gear, yet hard going. The dust was awful. At one time we got stuck behind a tank on a bad bit and you just got blinded every time we went round a bend, in a cloud of whiteness. You steered on slowly through the fog until you could see his silhouette again. There was a long stream of vehicles travelling North.

Not far South of Lentini, on a little plateau, we came across REME just off the road. Enquiries there led us to make for another REME unit near to Scordia, so, when we came through Carentini and down to Lentini by means of a most terrible by-road, we turned off the main road and made for Scordia. It was getting late and I was worrying about making camp before dusk, yet I wanted to find this REME to give us a clear day tomorrow. We pushed on through the Lentini strips past 239, 244 and 322 Wings and then it being dusk, and us rather lost, we pulled into camp as soon as we came out onto the main Scordia-Catania road, by a little railway station. I left the others there and went off for half an hour with Sgt. North, found the REME and gathered from their Colonel that he hadn't got a press after all, and that the only one he knew of would be with a colleague of his at Augusta. This was miles back near Syracuse on the coast. This press was as elusive as I feared it might be. I decided to spend tomorrow having a good look round North and reach Augusta by tomorrow night.

We had a grand meal in the dark; there was a full moon, luckily, and we slept the night on the ground all round the lorry with our mosquito nets tied to its sides. We pushed off early next morning and were in Catania by 08.30 hours.

I forgot; we had an invalid. Scottie had succumbed to a dose of what looked like malaria. He couldn't eat or stand up.

I was frightened of malaria but he wasn't shivering at all. So we put him on a bed in the back of the wagon, and there he lay all day. He recovered next day and served meanwhile as a guard for the lorry which we parked in the shade. We had a look round Catania for an hour or so on foot and again we were not impressed. Many of the shops had been broken into when the place was captured four days beforehand but we did no looting for there were too many civilians about, except that Roy struck lucky and got away with about a hundred camera films, size 120, a marvellous find.

I have been in Catania, at the RAF Hospital for a week or two since that time, and in describing my impression of the place will base it on that viewpoint rather than this superficial visit. Overall it seems a dirty, smelly battered town, top-heavy with many ornate public buildings, whose statues will have lost a head or an arm, and whose palatial insides may now be used for storing furniture, Fascist files and soldiers. Indeed it is a City of civilization broken down, and the messy result is horrible. Walking along a main street in their municipal quarter you may come across an exquisitely pansy uniformed Italian policeman directing traffic round a bombhole stinking of drains. At the side there will be a shop selling water ice-cream to British troops and next door the dusty remains of a rifled jeweller's shop, with opposite, the Town Hall, minus all its windows and with people queuing among its grotesque statues and piles of rubble for relief. The town may be divided into thirds: (1) The dock area, strictly military, with the usual barbed wire, sunken ships, African negro pioneers and furious lorries. Even in this case I think, a working railway line; (2) The municipal area, already described; (3) The residential area, inland and on higher ground, which is really quite pleasant in parts, containing wide, quiet, tree-lined streets with big houses on either side; but if you turn down a side street you soon came to lurking slums and garbage burning in the gutter.

After about half an hour we all re-embarked and it was decided to drive on up the North road to see if there was any Hun stuff left lying about as he retreated; but first I said "I want to see the authorities here about a piano. Only take ten minutes." It took about two hours before I gave up, furiously. Army Sub Area HQ said "No, they weren't organized enough yet." MP HQ said "Try CID". CID said "Oh yes, they knew where there were several pianos but, of course, they couldn't tell me unless I got a requisition order from Sub Area. Back to Sub Area with this news but "No", they had no authority to requisition pianos. "Try and hire one off some civilian through AMGOT." Down to AMGOT. "Oh yes, what's it for, a dance? Oh hmmmm. Well, come back tomorrow and I'll let you know." So I gave up. And I swore at the Army, at bureaucracy, and at Sub Area in particular, most feelingly.

We called in at a water point on the outskirts of the town and there while waiting in the queue had lunch. Then North again. There seemed to be a lot of traffic on the road but we did not notice really that it had changed from the usual RASC supply lorries and mixed other vehicles of all units, to all tanks and guns especially anti-tank guns.

After about fifteen miles we came to the small town of Acireale. There we crossed when our turn came in the long line; a blown up railway, drove up a street, round a corner and up another, cross country, marked on either side with white tape. Every soldier we noticed was now wearing his tin hat. There were many buildings destroyed and the whole place was mined and booby trapped. We suspected we had got too close to the battle for amusement, but we couldn't turn back, the road wasn't wide enough nor would I risk the mines. It was a ludicrous predicament, this gay RAF wagon mixed up in all these vicious proceedings. The soldiers waved to us to keep a good distance, they said that two lorries together would be shelled. There were snipers about, the shambled town otherwise deserted. It shook us rigid. It was with relief that I managed to pull out of the stream safely at the top of the hill. From there we could see RE's clearing mines and charging great bull-dozers about clearing rubble from the road. And there we were stuck for an hour waiting for the tide to turn. Eventually it did, and as we passed again the railway demolitions we asked someone how long the town had been in our hands. Twelve hours it appears. The line was held up just beyond it. We hurried off, South, on and on, through Catania and Lentini and made Augusta just at dusk where we befriended a Bofors gun battery and pitched blithely with them. That will be the last time I ever make camp among anti-aircraft guns, and in a port — from choice.

We thought we had done rather well. We had our evening meal cooked for us and sat round after dark pleasantly talking in a camp circle, with the gunners. Then we retired to bed, as ever round our wagon, which was parked a little way from any one gun, being in the middle of the field. Just as I was dozing off some guns opened up in the night. I woke up and heard the awful drone of aeroplanes, enemy bombers, invisible, close. Cursing, we all scrambled underneath the wagon and the din got louder. All the old night raid sounds, the booming of the big guns, the rat-tat-tat of the machine guns, the banging on pom-poms and cannon, and then the scream of a plane diving through the flak and the earth-shaking, crump, crump, of bombs landing. Sometimes there would come a whistle, growing louder as it neared the ground so that you would swear it was going to hit you, and then the explosion, miles away. Also there was, every now and again, quite apart from the gun firing and bombing, the rattle and whispering of shrapnel falling, bits of shells from the guns. From that the lorry protected us. One time a big piece came whistling down and landed about five yards away. It put an awful fear in us, we thought it was a bomb but it didn't go off and we found the bit of metal in the morning.

Fear made you want to dig into the ground with your fingers to get down, and to bury your head. And at the same time a sort of angry misery was there. Why should we have to run into this? When was it going to end? But most wonderful were the sights. A firework display was being given which almost made one forget fear in the watching of it. It was finer than Khemis, Bizerta or London. There were many ships in the port, and most of them warships. And the Navy had it all worked out. They did not use predictors, or shoot at anything, but just every gun they could muster on sea and on land was shooting altogether, each along a previously arranged line of fire. The result was a most comprehensive barrage over the whole area and at all heights. But what made it extraordinary was that all these guns used tracer ammunition for they were prepared for night or day work. So that from under our lorry you could look out from either side and see streams of red lights careering upwards in many straight lines. You could watch one red blob moving from the gun to ten thousand feet in a few seconds. It appeared to move slowly, at nearly 1,000 feet per second, straight up till it burst to extinguishment. And every now and again, in spite of and on top of all this, a series of flares would appear, silently, one after another and hang golden brilliant in the sky, lighting up the whole place so that our wagon cast a shadow over us. From them you might trace the course of an aeroplane, but, of course, as with the engine noise, it had long passed on. Lastly, there were the close flashes of our battery. As they fired their slow bursts, four or so shells at a time, there would be a succession of piercing flashes streak from the barrels of the guns, flash, bang, flash, bang, and so on; too close by, for the bombers were sure to see them too, we felt. But most wonderful were the millions of red needles tracing upwards.

The raid went on, as they appear to do, forever. It really lasted, I suppose, about two hours. Then we got some sleep.

Next morning all was sunlight and quiet. We drove into the small town of Augusta which is on a promontory and whose isthmus makes only one entrance to it. This entrance was guarded by the Navy, the town being closed, and we had to wangle an hour's pass to get in. Inside was a shambles. The place had been bombed by both sides and shelled heavily from the sea. There was not a civilian to be seen and indeed the streets of rubble were deserted except for an occasional Tommy or sailor or Redcap on patrol. I dropped everyone off to have a look round and went off with the wagon to a sea plane base where REME was. Yes, they had a press but it hadn't arrived yet, their transport coming by sea in a few days, so I arranged and left the blocks saying that they would be called for in about a week. Actually it was about a month before the job was done.

I drove back to Augusta and contacted the boys. Evidently this was a looter's Paradise. Every house and shop still standing had been plundered after the town was captured, though now, they said, things were under control, by closing the town evidently. It was deserted but we were inside. The boys had been having the time of their lives and their pockets were stuffed. Personally, I only wanted one thing and I asked if anyone had seen a piano. F/S Mann had, a good one, and it was down a side-street where there was no-one about. We debated whether to go to the town Major and ask his permission to take it but having talked to a Sgt. MP and discovered there was no Town Major and that the Provost Marshal took a serious view of such things (looting was a charge punishable by death) we decided to see if we could get away with it without risking a refusal and subsequent suspicion. We hoped we had fixed the Sgt. MP if we were caught by any of his men. Further, where pilots might get away with a thing like this, regular senior NCO's might not and also these four were all regulars with pensions to care for. So I later drove the ground crew members of the party out to the main gates of the town telling them we would pick them up on the road outside.

Now I left the others by the wagon and went to reconnoitre. While inspecting the house there was a noise from opposite in the otherwise deserted street. I was horrified to see two MP's looking out of an upstairs window, but then realised that it was me who had caught them doing a bit of quiet pilfering on their own. That fixed them. Everything else seemed clear. When I returned to the wagon, I found great consternation. We had unwisely left the wagon in the main Square by the PM's HQ. The Provost Marshal had evidently come along and seeing this suspicious looking vehicle with its Air Force personnel had wanted to know why and wherefore. The blokes had made some excuse about my engine blocks and the PM had warned them severely about looting. "If I catch any of you, you'll be shot," and wanted to see me when I got back. So we jumped on board and hurried off into a side street.

The deed was smoothly done. The pilots went ahead on foot, got the piano downstairs with great shushes, bumps and curses. I drove up fast with the tail-board down and a tent ready. Quickly we had the piano out of the front door, on its back, altogether with superhuman strength lifted onto the wagon, tent over, tail-board up, and away before anyone else saw us — except the two MP's opposite laughing. We drove gaily and with what were, we hoped, innocent expressions, through the guard at the main gate. Outside we picked up the four NCO's and much pleased with ourselves set off for home.

There was one more incident. We travelled fast and had reached Noto by about dinner time; it was, as ever a glorious morning and the movement kept off the heat. We were all in the best of spirits, only a few more miles to go. Sgt. North had taken over and I was in the back having a snooze when the lorry pulled up and two young Italian girls climbed on board. One got in the cab and the other in the back with us, both laughing and singing. Our one in the back promptly started flirting with everyone in turn and settled down to try and seduce Fergus. Now Fergus is rather serious where girls are concerned and reciprocated by practising Italian, which he was learning. Meanwhile she winked, laughed and sang at the rest of us, settling herself comfortably on Fergus's lap, to his surprise. He didn't know his Italian was so good.

Scottie, who had by now recovered, spent the time throwing grapes and epithets at her from the tail-board and Roy, who was sitting next to Fergus, came in for an embarrassing caress every now and again. The rest of us looked on, most entertained by this diversion and all the time we travelled on, bumping past sunlit orchards and vineyards. But evidently the girl in the front, having only two to contend with, had aroused greater passion for suddenly, having pulled up, North shouted out "Anyone else want to drive?" I took over again and Morris, who is young and a puritan in these matters, greatly shocked by the girl's advances to him while sitting on his knee, climbed into the back.

I realised as I let in the clutch that this seduction was meeting with more success than that of Fergus, for I was shaken by the sight of a pair of pink knickers on the floorboards. I hurriedly suggested that we stop at the next copse for a few minutes. This was heartily approved. North and his girl disappeared among the trees, while the rest of us had a bite to eat and a smoke. I could see Chiefy Mann, Roy and Scottie, eyeing the other girl suggestively, who was indeed the more attractive of the two, but none of us was sufficiently brazen to disregard the presence of the others and so she too ate, smoked, joked in Italian and played with Fergus. We took their photograph, his red face framed in billowing skirts and swarthy arms, and threatened to send it home to the girl he was often writing to, but it didn't come out. The other pair came back, North not walking with his usual spring and looking quite sheepish as they climbed up into the cab again. As we moved off a soldier on the other side of the road was astonished to see, in the front of a Military vehicle, a pair of bare legs and a blue skirt, flapping in the breeze. North blushed, the soldier waved enviously and Morris, from the back, summed up thoughtfully with "Well, that was the crudest thing I ever did see".

We dropped the two young ladies in Pachino and finally drove onto the aerodrome again about 3.00 o'clock on the third day.

A FEW WORDS ABOUT THE PIANO . . .

One day, or rather night, many months back, I had been visiting some of the blokes' tents after dark — an old Souk el Arba custom, though this was after we had moved to Khemis — with a view to finding out any suggestions for improving our way of living. Cpl Brown, an echelon Instrument Rep., suggested that a piano would be a good thing for the evenings. Several of the boys could play, he could tune one, and there might be sing-songs, etc. This seemed a good idea. I suppose that was about March. I thought it would be easy enough to get hold of a piano, and set about scrounging; but it wasn't. I sent lorries all over North Africa, different people on them picked for scroungers, to Bone, Constantine, Tunis, Bizerta,

Cape Bon, when the time came months later, for the matter was constantly in my mind. Cpl Jenkins got his hands on one in Bizerta but was then caught and nearly jugged as he was getting it out of the door, by MPs to whom it belonged. I met an Army Officer in Tunis and concluded all arrangements to take his unit's one over in a few days when they moved back to Algeria, but we moved off to Mateur first.

At Comiso again we had looked all over South East Sicily for one. By now the piano question had become a familiar joke among the men. My reputation rested on that over-confident promise given at Souk el Khemis, and there seemed no pianos to be had by any means — buy, hire, loan or loot. So it gave me keen pleasure that at last, not only had we got one, and a good one, but also that after all this effort, I had got it myself. With what a nonchalant air did I see it off the lorry and erect it in the airmen's mess, under a tree. But my pride burst when I met Cpls Brown and Jenkins and Charlie Evans. To "Jenks's" casual remark by the empty lorry "So you didn't get a piano sir," I burst out, "Oh yes we did!" and told them all about our adventures in Augusta. And they went off to admire it.

The piano became a boon. It came just at the right time. Never before had the squadron gone in for any sort of communal entertainment. There hadn't been time but now a series of concerts were started. Talent sprang up from all directions, other Squadrons were invited over to take part. It grew to such dimensions that Charlie, who organised and compèred the shows so ably, confided to me a dream of a mass concert of all five Squadrons and the Wing, staged at one end of the runway. Almost every letter I censored at that time mentioned these weekly concerts with great approval, many told Mothers and Wives about the piano, which some said the Engineer Officer had given them, like I was a fairy Godmother. Others said we had captured it and one even claimed that he had found it. But to most of them it was just there, like an Arab, a ship, or the Naafi ration.

As I left the Officers' Mess Tent after dinner one evening I heard in the distance the sound of voices singing. I walked up the slope and there, in the moonlight, in a great circle of dim shapes were men lying, sitting and standing. Here and there a cigarette glowed redly and a match lit up faces and a tree. A piano suggested a tune which was quickly taken up by many voices together. I recall some of the words —

"The other night, dear,
As I lay dreaming ......
I dreamt that you were by my side
But when I awoke dear
I was mistaken and held my head and cried "
I was repaid.

MOUNT ETNA   8-10-43

On 1st September, 1943, during the Squadron's moving period from Pachino to the North of Sicily and then to Italy, I had an accident with the 'Pisser', on a new strip near Gerbini. Danny and I had flown in there to have a look round preparatory to the Squadron's moving in. We had chosen the best dispersal area and returned to the Pisser to come home. Danny climbed into the front cockpit and I prepared to swing the propeller to start the engine which was the only way of doing it and which I had done many times before with Tom Hughes. "Contact" shouts I.

Once the engine had started, Danny waited for me to come aboard but when I failed to appear and the Pisser had rolled forward a little he slammed on the brakes and climbed out himself to have a look. He found me lying under the propeller completely unconscious, and quite bloody, as if the Pisser had simply mowed me down like a giant lawn mower. So he pulled me out and threw me into the rear cockpit and flew as fast as he could back to base. Seeing I was completely unconscious, the medics rushed me to No. 21 Field Hospital nearby. There I lay for two days still unconscious, in fact hovering between life and death. I had received a blow on the head from one of the spinning propeller blades just behind the right temple. I came to on the third day when I realized this was not where I ought to be and before the orderlies realized I was mobile, I went on a search to find someone I knew from 72 Squadron. There was nobody. I was still in a semi-coma and of course, the orderlies hurriedly got me back into bed. I lay there wondering what on earth could have happened in a sort of delirium for another two days before I could understand what the doctors were telling me; that I had quite a serious accident and not only the dangerous one to my head but also the second and third metacarpal bones of my right hand were broken and one tooth was missing from my upper jaw. I could remember absolutely nothing of all this; indeed from my having shouted, "Contact", there was a four day gap in my consciousness. Meanwhile a telegram had been sent to my mother saying that her son had been seriously wounded. The RAF are awfully good about notifying next of kin. Once I had come-to properly I thought to myself that with the total loss of memory, I might just as well never have come-to, i.e. died, and would never have known the difference.

As I recovered, the surgeons at No. 21 Mobile Field Hospital had a go at resetting the broken bones in my right hand. Maybe they had to do this to prevent them resetting themselves but in my opinion they did not make a very good job of it since the tendon to my fourth finger has remained too short ever since. However I am left handed anyway and have since found all sorts of uses for my bent finger. As soon as they felt i could be moved they passed me on to 11th General Hospital in Catania where I was examined for permanent neurosis and found OK. So then I was passed on again to the surgical unit of No. 25 Hospital for further attention to my right hand. While I was there a GI was brought in and put into the next bed to mine. He had turned over a Jeep and broken his neck. A succession of Padrés and adjutants came to see him during the few days he still had to live for it was a hopeless case, so I had to listen to his last messages to his family over in the US. I did not mind, I had just been luckier than him; one gets so hardened.

Then my hand went septic, just a mass of pus. The surgeon started to work on it when at the sight I suddenly fainted. The surgeon abruptly forced my head between my legs and called for a shot of morphine, which enabled me to regain interest in what he was doing to my hand. He was very skilful and soon had got rid of the pus while I enjoyed the morphine.

However, after antiseptics, they put on a cast so I had to go around with my arm in a sling for a month or two.

Everything now being on the mend I found myself posted to a most luxurious convalescent home for a very happy three weeks convalescence. It was really a classy hotel complete with waiters and waitresses which the RAF had requisitioned for the time being, half way up Mount Etna from where one could observe the Mediterranean on one side and the frozen lava streams all round us and it contained some of the most interesting characters I have ever met.

While all this was going on and unknown to me until later, an enquiry into what must have happened was being held. Danny was very straightforward; he admitted straight out that when I had shouted "Contact", he did not have the brakes on. This is a must on a Pisser unless one had chocks aboard which Tom and I never bothered with. Tom Hughes tried to take the blame for not having instructed Danny on this point but Danny simply brushed that aside and insisted on taking the blame himself. Of course when he did get out of the Pisser to find me he had to leave the engine running otherwise, we, being the only two people on the aerodrome, could never have started the Pisser again and for that exercise he certainly had to put the brakes on. I think he may have been absent minded the first time but undoubtedly his fast reaction the second time saved my life.

Coming back to my present heavenly conditions on the snow-line of Mount Etna at the classy hotel, I will describe it a bit. There was a library of a sort there and I read my way through about twelve books happily, among which I would mention "Ordinary Families" by E Arnott Robertson, and "I

Claudius", Volume I by Robert Graves. That book absorbed me. I couldn't stop reading and reading it and when I finished Vol. I quickly, suddenly I was left gasping for Volume II, the sequel "Claudius the God" which was not in this library. Volume I is an entrancing book of the Romans told in a personal style, which brings the portraits to life and the scenes and time within ken.

These two — both Penguins — were only a few of the many books I read in Hospital. I suppose I averaged one book every two days, that makes ten or eleven books but these are the only two I shall remember.

There are two other aspects of this Hospital life worth recording. One is the amount of information I picked up medically. I was fortunate in being a surgical case, for therefore I was fit enough, except for my hand, and could get about, and also I was lodged on the surgical side where from day to day many interesting cases came in. Also I made friends with the doctors, who were always ready to talk shop — about malaria, a complicated and interesting subject of which there were many examples in the hospital — about morphine, which I experienced with much pleasure — and bone surgery — and anaesthetising — and burns. It was all most interesting.

Then there was Mount Etna and the Albergo on its South side, half-way up to be exact. Built, contrasting to the tiled-floored and low many-windowed Sicilian houses, of thick walls, double windows parquet floors and central heating. We had double beds with spring mattresses, each to our own room with white and chromium bathroom attached. We were served and waited on by trained Italian staff. From the sunny esplanade in front of the Hotel one could look North to the top of the Volcano, its sides streaked with black lava streams of the 1890 eruption, or East out to sea, or South to the Plain of Catania, bound by the curving coast line and the Lentini Hills in the distance, or West towards pinewoods in which I loved to roam and below them little white and pink towns at the foot of the central mountains.

Here in this place there was assembled a number of RAF Officers, drawn from different and various sections of the RAF; pilots from Spitfire and Kittyhawk Squadrons, a navigator from Bostons, Desert Staff Officers, a Senior Intelligence Officer, an Engineer Officer and a RAF Nursing Sister, all convalescing and for some reason, I suppose as a result of the environment and the different points of view, we used to get talking, usually during a meal time, and such interesting conversation, discussion or story telling would ensue that the talk spontaneously would go on sometimes right through from lunch to tea, at the dining table. I shall always remember that convalescence for these good talks, and I realised that the RAF was not just a Spitfire Squadron.

Of people, I made friends with two in particular, the 'Colonel' who was a South African Air Force Lieutenant, and W/C Wiseman. The 'Colonel' was a navigator in a medium Bomber Squadron and a South African. He was suffering from deafness due to having flown with a cold. They said it was temporary. He didn't know, and every day on our walks, he used to say how much better his hearing was today, and so I would shout even louder. Finally, one ear got better. Bags of joy. And a week later the other. He caught the surgeon in the middle of a dance and next day was on the way back to his

Squadron. He told me of air navigation and how if his pilot was young and cocky, he would let him lose himself and then bring him home. And of the 'Cape' and his job as Secretary of a big engineering works in South Africa.

Wiseman was a young man, and is currently the Senior Intelligence Officer in Tactical Air Force. He had been a classical student of London and Cambridge; he was an eminent archaeologist who believed in Genesis. He spoke French and German fluently. He was one of the most interesting conversationalists I have ever met. In the RAF since the War, he had risen from P/O at North Weald and had been Personal Assistant to Air Vice Marshal Keith Park (whom I saw in Malta) when he was Air Officer Commanding 11 Group during the Battle of Britain; he had flown many hours in night fighters during the Blitz developing AI (Airborne radar detection) although he was not officially air crew; he had been on the planning staff at Air Ministry and above all he had been one of the five Staff Officers (of whom W/C Maggs was another) controlling the Air Forces during the North African invasion; and so on to TAF. We had North Africa in common and I let him read this diary, which practical point of view of a Squadron Engineer Officer interested the Staff Officer enormously in their common experience. We talked and talked for his talk interested me enormously. He told stories of the back-room boys, of the Souk el Arba period. I saw the reasons for many of the amazing happenings of that time, especially in respect of our isolation from support. He talked of Khemis, the Thelepte 'do', Malta, Comiso, and the Sicilian invasion. Of the Salerno beaches and the new Hun 'flying bomb', and of interrogating prisoners.

He related the inside story of the Dieppe show; how there was no leakage of information and that its aim was to test the German coastal defence for future planning and how strong the defence was. He described what London looked like from the air during a big night Blitz, and how, during the Battle of Britain, Churchill used to ring up the Ops room at Uxbridge several times a day for the latest score.

He discussed archaeological proof of Genesis against Darwin; the Le Kef Roman ruins at Hydra (between Tebessa and Le Kef) and the Roman method of colonization; translating Etruscan writings; and civilisations of early times, the Syrian and Phoenician.

He criticised everybody and everything around him. He pulled the Doctors' legs, flirted all day with the nurses and made friends with everyone equally, Group Captains and AC2. He was that most entertaining companion, an intellectual and a simple man.

While convalescing, I received the following letter from Danny:

Ref: 72S/C.251/2/P3   No. 72 (Basutoland) Squadron
Royal Air Force
Central Mediterranean Force
11th September, 1943

Dear Spanner,

I am writing to you to tell you that on the instructions of Desert Air Force we have had to post you non-effective from the old squadron and that when you are fit again you are <u>not</u> to return direct to this unit but are to report to Rear Air Headquarters Desert Air Force.

Now I dont want you to worry about this. When you are on your feet again let me know as quickly as you can and I will then see what can be done about you returning to "Seventy-Two".

I'm sure I dont need to tell you how dreadfully sorry I am about your accident, and I can tell you that the whole Squadron misses you – and your funny ways! You've done a grand job with the squadron and it is greatly appreciated. Your job now is to do as the doctors tell you and to get well as quickly as possible.

In the meantime it seems that we need <u>Two</u> men to fill you shoes. We got a W/O. and now a young P/O.

That I think is all for now. Once more wishing you a speedy recovery and that we shall meet again before long.

I am,
Yours sincerely,
Danny

F/O. H G Farish (63124)
c/o. 11th General Hospital.

I thought of many things,
Of the sudden beauty of moving scene,
Of memory, yearning back to an environment,
Of the fight of the spirit of little men
and the crack Squadron that came of it; then
The loss, and the thanklessness of authority.
But I thought of the little men. They thanked inertly.
Only I realized wholly the battle, always to be lost,
Yet always won; in the inert instinctive appreciation
Of their unspoken thanks.

After two days at Foggia, return by air and spent a day in Salerno before arriving at my new Squadron. Thus for four nights running, having come straight out of Hospital, I was on the road, travelling light, sleeping anywhere, weather wet and cold. This was the usual experience of men returning from hospital to duty.

Foggia was the worst shambles I have yet seen of a town. As a result of Allied bombing, continuously, there were few building left, and no windows. I saw one shop, just opened, a tailor's shop it was.

Desert Air Force, a Head Quarters Unit full of Staff Officers who could choose where they like to live and work, was located miles from anywhere, in a field under canvas. Good old 'Desert', Naples, Bari, etc., full of marvellous office buildings and flats, and central, but that would not occur to them. In the Officer's Mess there, I went into dinner in shorts and shirt but hurriedly retired again to put on a tie and slacks.

This morning driving from the Mess (we live in two pleasant houses in the Town) to the aerodrome, which is on the edge of the plain above the city near the foot of Vesuvius, I passed through 'tharsands and tharsands' of Italians all walking out. Just one long continual stream of people choking the roads, family by family. It was the same at all the exits of the town. Today there is a general exodus of the City's population, on foot, for they have no other transport.

The reason for this is because the electricity is coming on today. Since the battle for the city, about a month ago, there has been no light but candles, for of course, the Germans demolished the Power Station. Now it has been rebuilt and some of the generators repaired. When they switched on the mains at Salerno, in much the same circumstances, a few mines exploded here and there. Hence gossip and rumour has taken such a hold on these people that the authorities must announce that the mains will be switched on between the hours of ten and twelve and the people take refuge. I don't think any mines went off in Naples; there had been a thorough search after the Salerno experience.

Our Wing is now located on the Naples City Civil 'drome, a vast grass expanse surrounded by smashed hangars and houses, on the edge of the town to the north and abounding in the most lovely views of Spitfires standing on green sward at the foot of Mount Vesuvius. Everyone lived in billets, houses in the town, which is the first time we have been fixed so, and private cars were requisitioned, right and left. We settled down to play this run of luck to the limit, for the Army was not moving forward very fast and the enemy air activity was negligible and we were in the most comfortable and interesting external circumstances yet presented. Thus I shall describe our life at Naples a little. It is divided into two parts, work — on the aerodrome, back to the Mess for meals and down to the men's block of flats for the MT yard, so that I am always tearing about in the jeep which I have had covered in, so that it is wind and rain-proof, with materials from an old tent, some tubing and perspex, for the Winter.

The aerodrome, as I have said, is on the North East edge of the town. It is of course, the City Air Port, and although already it has had consecutive days of rain, it has never been unserviceable. It is called Capodichino. It has a large expanse of grass and all round this a concrete perimeter track. Beyond this again, on three sides, were built hangars, office blocks, garages, etc., and on the East side is a wood. There are houses outside all the way round. Of the hangars, we found all but one (I suppose there were about fifteen) so well demolished by our previous bombing and Jerry's more scientific methods, as to be useless. On the grass, scattered in all directions are aeroplanes. The Spitfires of 324 Wing, DC3's of the American transport people, a Squadron of Air Observation Austers, a Squadron of Army Co-op Spits and all sorts of many nationalities. Beyond all and overlooking the flat aerodrome to the South is Mount Vesuvius, so that always one can see it, changing colour with cloud and sun and time, sometimes topped in cloud, always smoking white and at night, from time to time, a glowing red ball at the summit.

In addition to the aerodrome there are sections of the Wing and Squadron scattered all about Naples in old buildings so that we are more widely dispersed now than ever, but for reasons of comfort rather than discretion. Notably, our Officers Mess is in one part of the town, a slummy part, but in two quite pleasant houses in a group set apart. Wing Sick Quarters is about half a mile up the street towards the aerodrome; '72' billet is about two miles down the street. The big block of flats in which our airmen and those of '93' live, with the MT yard behind, lies to the South of the aerodrome, quite near, and on the edge of a sort of escarpment, so that from them there is a marvellous view of the City, and the bay right round past Pompeii, to Sorrento and the Isle of Capri.

Over all these places we work. And then there is play. See Naples and die. Yes, and be there and live. What shall I describe? Lunching in the sun at a little restaurant which lies on a point around the bay, so that from it you can look across the blue water where the sails of fishing boats bob up and down; at the city, flashing, towering, moving; and beyond it, at the volcano benevolently blowing smoke rings through its white plume. You can watch the colours changing on the sides as a cloud passes across the sun, or you can watch the fishermen bringing their catch at your feet, which, if approved, may be cooked for your meal. A big ship may be manœuvering into the port, or an airliner circling the aerodrome, on top of the town. And to the music of a violin you may eat clams, fried octopus, boiled fish, roast veal with French fried potatoes, and bags of olive oil, with a white wine called Lacrima Christi to wash it all down. The wine is grown on the fertile volcanic soil of the lower skirts of Vesuvius.

Or shall I describe dancing at a night club, called "*Il Giardino degli aranci*", or something like that? Dancing to a black band on a crowded postage stamp floor among many uniforms, lit by red, blue and green indirect lighting, eating ice cream, drinking cognac, and for company a pretty nurse. Perhaps you may see Naples, like a bridal train beneath you, for this place is on a height. One night I was there when sirens wailed shortly of air raiders coming. As the whistling died away great billows of white smoke rose up in a semi circle round the front, and spread across leeward slowly, so that soon the Docks, the water and the shops were covered by a screen of cumulus, which looked like cotton wool. Out of this rose the dark mass of Vesuvius and like a beacon at the top, a red glow came and went as it puffed away. A fairyland, I wished the raid would materialise for we were far enough away and I wanted to see the tracer barrage, the flares and the bomb flashes. But it didn't — only the smoke screen made getting home like crossing Hyde Park in a November fog.

Or shall I describe driving through the large cobble stone streets, past shops with broken blinds of tin, and dodging the population? It takes half an hour to get up the Via Roma, a main street of about a mile in length, at noon time, what with ambulances, lorries, jeeps, Italian taxis, tattered wagons and horse- and hand-carts, let alone the crowds of people overflowing the side-walks and crossing the street disregardingly. I think Neapolitan old ladies must be the finest jay-walkers in the world.

The shops were comparatively bountiful when we first came into the city; I have bought a slide rule, a propelling pencil, a Longines watch, a pipe, a tobacco pouch, a flashy shirt, an embroidered silk shawl and a dozen roses (for 5 shillings) and a new lens for my glasses. But now they are nearly stripped by all the visiting soldiers, though there are still some things in the old little pedestrian side streets, and, of course, bags of barber's shops everywhere. Italians have their hair cut every day, and by a hair cut, I mean a cut, wave, shampoo, shave with refinements like up your nostrils and in your ears, finished off with oils, perfumes and even powder.

Or shall I describe our Officers' Mess? About twenty-five young men let loose with money, time, transport, in a recently captured city. Wine, women and song with a vengeance. Almost every night, until far into the morning, there is a party. Wine, spirits, and for the first month beer, overflowed. The songs, "Lilli Marlene", "Sunshine", "Red Wing", "From Khemis to Medjez", etc. ad infinitum, in drunken chorus, accompanied by a clarinet and concertina, with, towards the end, drumbeats of broken furniture. The women — hardly a night passed without some woman being in one bed or another. We used to sleep three or four in a room and at first, if a member was entertaining a local beauty or a nurse, he would ask the other occupants of his room not to come to bed until such and such hour. But later on, nobody bothered with formalities. It seemed that the women were trying their best to repopulate the stricken world as fast a possible; they could not help themselves. Such was life in Naples. A fantasy of war and peace. We came into the city in September, dirty in our lorries and in tropical kit. We left it — to go under canvas again — not long after Christmas.

DISPERSAL POINT NOON – CAPODICHINO   19-12-43

Sitting in the sun on the step of our Operations caravan surrounded by maps of Italy and coloured boards, showing serviceability and who's flying where. There is much activity on the 'drome, Spit squadrons taking off and landing continuously. I am acting as Intelligence Officer for George Usher who is ill, besides my job of putting the aircraft up. At 11.25 our boys, who were on readiness, were scrambled. Seven went off, all Spitfire V's, one extra by mistake. Frantic phone calls for more pilots for six IX's were due to take off on a sweep at 11.35. Sent wagons off to get Sergeants and Officers from the Messes, then got the R/T relayed through to me on the telephone. Listened in to 'Mac' leading Red Section and Jim leading Black, as they patrolled over the front, looking for Bandits. Meanwhile, all the flight men grouped round, in a big semi-circle listening too. Mac's voice "Aircraft below you to port Jim", and Jim's voice "Yes, I see him, going in". Great excitement. Then the pilots turned up for the next show late, and so much activity getting them off. 'Banker Blue' joined in over the R/T with 'Steamer', 'Packard', 'Ratter'. Mac's voice "Hullo, Changer, Banker Red calling, I can see nothing here" and the controller answered that they were to return to base.

    Jim didn't get anything. The aircraft was friendly and they saw no enemy aircraft. I am still sitting here, in a warm winter sun, basking in the beauty of the Neapolitan scene and Spitfires flying, and listening to the short excited voices of the pilots, English and Americans, in the enemy air.

DIARY ENTRY MADE IN 1945: TOM HUGHES MISSING 24-12-43 AND FOUND 10-2-45

I remember, nearly a year ago, that is about February 1943, one day in the little house by the railway line which we used as a Mess at Khemis, two new pilots arrived, both new to operational flying. One, Scrase his name, very young, very talkative, was just finished training. The other was Tom Hughes. He was quiet, especially reluctant to mention himself, but when he did talk, if only a few words, one heard a beautiful voice, speaking pure English. He had a healthy, ordinary, rather spotted, face, with a nondescript shock of brown hair above it. Only wrinkles which could come across his forehead and the power of his shoulders, shewed this schoolboy to be a man.

They looked at his Log Book and found that he had done over a thousand hours flying, already more than anyone else on the Squadron. He was passed as a 'Q' Instructor at the Central Flying School, the highest qualification a pilot can get in the RAF and a rarity in wartime. And he had many types. Most of them had flown Tiger Moths, Masters and then only Spitfires, to which, from my memory Tom could add Harvards, Hurricanes, Oxford, Blenheims, Beaufighters. He had only recently come on to fighters having been an Instructor at a Night Fighter Beaufighter and Blenheim twin engine aircraft Operational Training Unit (OTU). He had an Engineering background and so took Pete Fowler's place as my test pilot; he would come down after landing and modestly take much trouble to understand what we might be testing and to explain symptoms of what might be wrong. Indeed he was mad on flying, on flight, the air; he lived for that incomprehensible singleness, flying, and he knew more about it than anyone I had ever met; yet if he could, he learned something more every day for he was interested in anything appertaining to aeroplanes.

One day at Khemis, 'Pryth' came in off a sweep, just before dusk (as I have already related on 12-3-43), and said Tom had force-landed on the other side of a ridge of mountains to the South. I set out to look for him with LAC McCaul from the Orderly Room who could read the stars and we didn't stop till, finding the kite next morning with the help of some friendly Arabs, I heard that Tom had walked into the Mess just after lunch. By this time Danny was flying over and dropping us messages. Tom had tried to cross the mountains in the dark without a light, fallen down a ravine, nearly died of exposure, nothing to drink, and he was unconscious in a delirium when the Doc put him in bed. The first words he said when he saw me were, "Thank you Spanner, for looking for me", and later when confirmed that the cause of the crash was that the throttle control had parted in the engine, "then there was nothing I could have done to get back?" Several months after this experience he told me that he hadn't made water for two days due to the dehydration but within forty-eight hours he was back flying on operations.

The months went by, the Tunisian campaign finished. Tom hadn't shot any down, I think he had a 'damaged', and although he had flown many operational hours, he showed none of the common signs of pilots of being tired. He never came back early off shows for imaginary reasons, was always keen, his flying did not deteriorate. He became most popular and sincerely respected by everyone. He would go far out of his way to do anything, big or mean or 'littly kind' for anyone. He did not seem to have a self.

We moved to Malta, there I used to go out sailing with him, we finding a common interest in the red-sailed Sharpe dinghy. Sailing across Buzzebugia Bay in the sun's brightness, or swimming from the boat in turns, we used to talk sometimes. Once we talked of shooting Huns down. He discussed it, fighting in the air, as a science, deeply thought out. He said that some people, like Danny and George Keith, were fitted by character to be fighter pilots. Even Joe Scrase, with his boyish ways, would fight like a demon when in a tight corner. There seemed to be a certain absoluteness, or concentration about it, besides the ability to shoot straight, to watch your own tail, to avoid tactical enemy traps, and not to follow a Hun down. Tom was worried about it, he pointed out that he couldn't seem to shoot them down; perhaps he was so fine a flyer that he could not hamfistedly throw a kite about like Chas Charnock did until it broke; he couldn't purposely side-slip in a turn to keep his gun sights on a target.

I told him about Keith Kuhleman and his success after a slow analysis of the art of fighting until he had it all cold bloodedly at his finger tips. There was another type of fighter pilot.

When the Sicilian invasion occurred and once again operations became intensive; on that marvellous day in Malta when the squadron shot down 13, Tom got one; I was so glad. Then we moved in to Sicily.

At Comiso we picked up, as I have related before, a Caproni Moth, and an Me 109. I myself did a lot of flying in the Caproni with Tom, culminating in our famous plane-to-lorry message passing with Cpl Jenkins at Carlentini. Also he used to arrange for pilots to take the ground crews up for flips in the Moth as much as possible. The echelon, who looked after the plane and who compose the highest trade groups, being particular as skilled tradesmen are, considered Tom their pilot and indeed some of them wouldn't go up with anyone else but him.

But the Messerschmidt, though it didn't start out that way, became essentially Tom's enterprise. While we were checking it over in the echelon, camouflaging it and finding out where to put oil, glycol, petrol, and what all the nobs did, besides finishing off the repairs the Germans had been working on, Tom went around finding out all he could about it. He talked to the Americans and learned how to fly it. He experimented and thought till he found what everything in the cockpit was for, and he translated, with the help of a dictionary, all the German instructions in the aircraft into English.

Danny actually flew it first, after I had personally ground tested the engine, because he was CO, and how it wasn't pranged I do not know. He swung all over the place on take off and landing, bounced so far, so often, that he used the whole of a 2,000 yard runway to get it down. Tom flew it beautifully — he said it was a fine aeroplane. He flew it on some trials with Spits and instructed the few other pilots who tried it, and when we moved to Pachino it was Tom who brought it across to the strange rough landing ground safely. Then one evening, at Pachino, Sexton Gear took it up and got mixed up in a barrage of our own ack-ack fire over the 'drome. He had omitted to warn the gunners or to have a Spit escort. While we all lay on the ground waiting for the 109 to be shot down with Sex in it, a man ran out to a Spitfire, climbed in, started up and took off, just like that. He flew into the flak, low through the machine guns' fire, then circled higher and weaved gently above Sex amid the bigger shell bursts. As the Spit slowly waggled its wings over the Me 109 on the circuit the ack-ack fire subsided and finally ceased and Sex came in to land, much shaken but otherwise unhurt though unfortunately he fogot to lock down one undercarriage leg. It was Tom Hughes in the Spit. He had no helmet, no gloves, no parachute nor straps. Meanwhile George Keith had been killed before either his DFC, or the bar to it, had come through. Sex had got a DFC and Danny a Bar to his. Roy Hussey had the DFM and Sgts. Connolly, Morris, and "Scottie" were all putting up the Squadron's score. Tom's second stripe came through and he became a Flight Lieutenant.

Tom had one more adventure before he left us. He was testing out another 109 which the Americans had given us. On its first flight, having climbed to about 2,000 feet after take off, evidently a glycol pipe burst, for he was smothered in glycol in the cockpit. He said he couldn't breathe so he had to bale out. I was watching the air test rather anxiously and when I saw the parachute suddenly appear in the clear sky and the Messerschmidt diving to destruction, I got rather excited. Tom had landed in a vineyard, without mishap, and I found him riding home with a peasant on a picturesque Sicilian two-wheeled cart, parachute and all. He admitted later that he was glad that it had happened, for it was one more experience of the air. And it was a special jump, out of an enemy aircraft, rather unusual for the Caterpillar Club.

Then a vacancy occurred in 43 Squadron for a Flight Commander. Of all those available, Tom was by reputation now the obvious choice. 43 Squadron was another crack squadron like 72 and led by a Polish Ace named Horbacz-ewski. I suppose we all have our idols. Horby became Tom's idol just as mine was Tom himself. It did not take Tom long to learn from Horby what had been wrong with his shooting technique; Tom had not been allowing enough lead for the time the bullets take to leave the guns and reach the target. Very shortly Tom's score began to mount and he was awarded the Distinguished Flying Cross. Then a vacancy occurred for a Flight Commander on 72 Squadron again and Danny asked for, and got back, Tom to lead the flight. This meant that 72 Squadron now had three 'dead-eye dicks' leading them. Danny as leader, Tom on the left four and Roy Hussey on the right. Roy was a special case too; he had started as a Sergeant Pilot way back, won the Distinguished Flying Medal (reserved for outstanding NCO pilots) and gained promotion to Commissioned Rank in the field on the recommendation of Bobby Oxspring. With experience his score kept mounting and before long he was awarded the Distinguished Flying Cross as an officer, in addition to his DFM. His reputation among the pilots was not as high as Tom's since Tom never forgot his Number 2 behind him, whereas Roy would occasionally go after a kill leaving his Number 2 exposed.

But the most remarkable thing about Roy Hussey was his ability to survive. The normal tour of duty for a pilot was officially 200 hours, but the CO could always extend this some. Indeed Bobby extended his own tour of duty too long for himself and one day found he could not bring himself to take off. That was when Danny had to take over the Squadron.

People not leading Squadrons have no idea of the stress involved and Bobby had been leading squadrons since the Battle of Britain with a marvellous reputation for not losing his junior pilots. He also had a wonderful power of delegation throughout the Squadron Personnel too, having promoted LAC Mike McCaul from junior clerk in the Orderly Room to Intelligence Officer and then not stood in his way when McCaul went on to higher responsibilities with 'Tiny' at Wing Headquarters before being taken ill at Pachino and being evacuated to 5 RAF Hospital at Heliopolis. In due course and after a Medical Board, he was posted as a Commissioned Officer to Baghdad for intelligence duties. After the war, he joined MI5 and rose to receive a CMG before he retired. The reader will recall that even as an LAC, Mike McCaul had volunteered to come with me to look for Tom after he had crash-landed in the mountains south when we did not know exactly where the lines between us and the Germans lay.

To come back to Roy Hussey, he never showed the normal signs of fatigue and kept shooting down enemy aircraft as well as ever, so his tour of duty was extended from 200 hours, firstly to 400 hours, and then on to 450 as Flight Commander.

Finally HQ insisted on his having a rest so he was sent home to England for a soft job testing Mustangs off the Vicker's assembly line. Maybe someone in Vickers made a mistake on assembly shortly thereafter and on test, Roy crashed in flames before the war was over. I never heard of anyone else doing 450 continuous hours of operational flying. That left Danny and Tom leading the Squadron while they trained a new Flight Commander. Now Tom was also, like Roy, one of those pilots who never showed signs of fatigue or distress so one tended to take him for granted. In December 1943 Tom was leading his flight as usual when he called up on the radio and said "Don't worry about me, boys; I am going back to argue it out with Challenger (the Controller)", and he turned by himself out of formation. Another curious point, while he was walking out to his aircraft before the sweep he had said to Barney, "Look, if I don't come back, you'll take over, won't you?" Barney did not know what to make of this remark so just nodded, but he remembered it enough to report it to the Intelligence Officer.

The following, in Tom's own words, was supplied in 1994:

"The other sweep was led by Flying Officer Barnfather. They were told to be at 1,000 feet over the Bay of Naples to rendezvous with a squadron of American Mustangs who had not yet turned up. Such delay was vital since every minute our engines were consuming petrol and a Spitfire only had enough fuel for about one and a half hours flying time. Suddenly, my engine became very rough. I told Barnfather that I would have to go back. It was a real fault of some sort and enough to cause me to think that I did not want to be over water – I handed over with a wiggle of wings and a brief word on the radio to Barnfather and dived back towards Capodichino.

"It might well have been the aneroid because as soon as I got low down to 2,000 feet or so, the engines became quite smooth. So, why not go north and see what I could find north of the battle? I climbed north and took a dive at great speed (500m mph) over the smoke of the monastery of Monte Cassino and suddenly saw the dreaded white golf balls coming up – so I pulled up and the engines stopped. I was hit and the propeller stopped. I wheeled and swung. I got the hood off by pushing the Jefferson and the canopy flew away. I quickly dived towards the earth north of the monastery. Everywhere there were rocks; no meadows in sight. I skimmed along the ground as low as I could.

"I woke up to find I was in a room in Rome. We were taken to Merano (in the Italian Tyrol) for Christmas 1943. I had burnt legs and had been hit in the head by the aircraft. There was a series of terrible journeys in Germany until I arrived at hospital in Winnenden, 15 miles north-east of Stuttgart, where I was kept for quite some time. there were a great many traumas in Hospital."

What Tom meant by trauma can best be illustrated by an actual case which he described. The front line Germans were comparatively decent men and must have been those who pulled him out of his burning aircraft, so saving his life. But it was, at this late stage of the war, the custom for captured pilots to be handed over to prison camps run by the German High Command, probably because so many pilots escaped. One of Tom's experiences at Winnenden prison camp was as follows:

"I lay on my German psychiatrical bed at Winnenden completely exhausted. I had fought all night but finally the

German sanitators had won. They had penetrated my anus to my large intestine and flooded my bowels with formaldehyde. I woke with a pile of faeces around my testicles. The daily inspection by Professor Doctor Krohle was taking place. He stopped by my bed. "How goes it my fighter boy?" With a lightning leap I had him. I smeared his sparkling white and silver uniform with my own SHIT. I had won my war! His iron cross I missed! Dear Herr Professor Kroele could have had me shot but I was moved back into solitary confinement. I was served afternoon tea with bone china on a tray; I was nearly over the border. But eventually the Swiss Red Cross Commission came and I was told I would be exchanged for three Germans at the Swiss border in a month or so's time. Another frightful train journey because of the bombing, and finally I arrived at the border near Constance and from there into Switzerland on February 10, 1945. Train to Marseilles and boarded the "Arundel Castle" arriving at Liverpool docks on February 17."

Tom had been held in POW hospitals for 14 months. He had, of course, been posted "Missing Believed Killed" until he turned up in Constance. Tom was the last English pilot exchanged during the war.

In civilian life Tom got an Honours degree at Cambridge in Electro-Mechanical Engineering, served a full and interesting career with various Engineering Companies and is now enjoying retirement in Northumberland. I met him for a short while in March 1994 when he gave me the leather-backed wings which he usually wore in action. These wings originally belonged to a Canadian pilot named Cameron. The reason for this wonderful compliment will become apparent in the next chapter.

When the Wing moved back from Naples to the little wooded island strip on the north bank of the Volturno river by the sea, the Squadrons in 324 Wing (other than 72 who had them a long time, since the Tunisian campaign in fact) were at last being equipped with Spit IX's. 111 Squadron had to wait their turn a bit because they were the first squadron to receive a new mark of Spit IX powered by Merlin 66 engines, specially designed for low flying at high speed.

We received our first Spit IX's on January 17th. I was pleased about this, once again to handle the first of a new type, and we all set to with great interest. But we ran head first into trouble. It went on and on, bad troubles, silicone deposits appearing on the plug tips and shorting them out was the worst, then water in the petrol filters and oil coolers bursting. All the time we had to keep level on operational commitments with the other squadrons who had Spit IX's with Merlin 63 engines, well proven by now. The flying was all out again, covering the new beach-head at Anzio, to which the Germans had also brought down Messerschmitts from the North. They didn't intend for us to capture Rome by going round the back door of Monte Cassino and rapidly threw a strong perimeter around Anzio which the American 5th Army was unable to pierce.

At first the Americans laid down a pierced steel plank air strip right alongside the beach called Nettuno, on which they stationed their own Squadron of Spitfires. But the Germans soon spotted this and brought up long range guns which put the airstrip well within their range. They shelled away and soon the southern part of the strip became a mass of crashed aeroplanes; unusable, until on the 15th February, the Americans had to abandon the airstrip as an operational base and it became an emergency landing ground only. Towards the end of this period however, as will be related later, the American ground crews became very resistant to working out on the strip because of the constant shelling.

After about three weeks of this, just managing to keep a squadron up, I heard from the ground crews at Gela that water had been found in the B Flight bowser. This necessitated recalling three kites off a sweep, one of which didn't come home directly but force-landed on the Nettuno strip, but got back eventually. I gave B Flight hell for not cleaning their bowser conscientiously (for this could always happen) but found I was being unfair when the very next day some water was found not only again in B Flight bowser but also in that of A Flight, just before the boys were going off on a show. I grounded the lot, which had to be done but did not make me very popular with Wing Operations, while we set to to drain the bowsers again and clean out all the aircraft fuel filters.

We could not guess where the water was coming from; no other squadrons were having water trouble and all the bowsers drew their supply from the same source, but we were now satisfied our bowsers were pretty clean. The day after that the weather was bad so a conference of senior officers on the squadron was held at which two local Rolls representatives were present. As yet nobody associated the water traces which must have been getting into the engines in spite of the petrol filters, with the silicone deposits on the spark plugs. Nobody knew at that stage what was really the matter and all the conference could come up with was to widen the gaps in the spark plugs, which was done without its making any detectable difference. The Rolls Royce technical representatives realized that our problem was outside of their range and wisely called in Rolls Royce Derby, for help from the experts there who had designed and developed the engine. It would naturally be several days before these experts could be rounded up and brought to Southern Italy. so now the squadron had been grounded on two occasions for technical problems which would surely set the alarm bells ringing.

It is rare for a squadron to be grounded except for weather. We had lost one 'kite' and pilot over enemy territory early on – Prytherch – although the actual cause of his engine failure was unknown. It was a miracle that we didn't lose more. I was worried to death, almost every day we had one or two Spits down on the Anzio beach-head strip at Nettuno, force-landed. They all got back sooner or later. All but one, 'A', so while the rest of the Squadron were flying as usual, I was afraid every minute to hear of a crash or force-landing somewhere, knowing what I did about the state of the aircraft. Freddy Charters, a reliable pilot, flew our old Spit V up to the beach-head to give Bamby Taylor some plugs from me for 'A', and I expected to see them both back, the V and the IX, that evening. But Freddy came back at noon. He was shaken. He told his story in front of many of the pilots at dispersal – which allowing for exaggerations – came to three points:

1)   the landing strip was under shell fire

2)   the Americans had evacuated the 'drome

3) Bamby could get no one to work on his aircraft and the strip was becoming unserviceable with shell holes and crashes.

Freddy had had to clear a crash himself, with Bamby, to get away. The boys were just going off on another show and just before he took off the CO said to me, in his meaningful but kind way, "Well, it looks as if we have had 'A'".

So then a wild scheme came into my head. I had a pretty good idea what was wrong with 'A'; plugs or water, and I reckoned I could fix it, and with any luck get Bamby away. The only thing to do was to go up there, but getting there was the problem and had been to me all that week. The Nettuno strip was on a beach head, just south of Rome, with the enemy all round it and south down to Gaeta point on the 5th Army front.

The only way was to fly there, and the only aeroplane available was the old Spitfire V. To begin with, you can't ask anybody to take you to a place like that in a 'Pisser' and there were only two 'Pissers' – that of the 31st F Group (USAAF), whose I had already had refused early in the week, and the Group Captain's, whose was private property and he would not allow it near front lines. Added to these things, I had worked as an Engineering Officer on Spitfires for three years and, of course, had seen only too many of our pilots killed for one reason or another.

Living with the pilots in the mess was a great privilege, even when one lost a good personal friend. Indeed it was perhaps wise, being a ground officer, not to become too friendly with the pilots in general. But how could one avoid that with people like Tom Hughes, Sexton Gear and Charles Charnock; the latter having been shot down three times in Africa and walked back through the lines every time with the discreet help, both of the gold Louis that were sewn (as escape money) into his tunic and, once, his revolver, to force the loan of a donkey. He was expert at disguising himself as an Arab.

It would not be untrue to say that without showing it, I loved and worshipped all pilots. I was then only 24 years of age and being rather short-sighted was ineligible for flying duties. But from half way through the war onwards, how I wished that I had managed to become a pilot myself. In a way I was a walking time bomb: I had for years said to myself that if ever an occasion arose when it would be cowardly not to try flying myself, then I would try. And now an extraordinary combination of circumstances seemed to have arisen which made it incumbent to get Bamby Taylor off the shell-ridden airstrip at Nettuno before he got killed due to <u>my</u> engine letting him down: or so it seemed to me. I could hardly back out now and retain my own self-respect.

Thus, without really deciding on the plan but in a distraught state, I told F/S Ratcliffe to "box up the DI on 'U', it might be going up in twenty minutes". He said it was overdue for inspection and made me sign up for an extension for this urgent flight (EO's responsibility), which I did rather with my tongue in my cheek. Then I contrived to get a map, parachute and Mae West out of the operations lorry, borrowed some tools off Sgt.

Trailing in 'A' Flight and asked Carl what the landing speed of a Spit was, the only point I was doubtful about. F/S Ratcliffe started worrying me about some bright scheme of his for stopping his oil coolers bursting. I bit his head off and walked away. Then I thought, I couldn't do it, and again, how often I had thought of what I would do in such an emergency as this – I couldn't betray myself and fighter pilots now. So I drove the jeep over to 'U' with all the gear in it and proceeded to don parachute and Mae West and climbed into the cockpit. It says much for the discipline I kept among my men that the Flight Mechanics who strapped me in did not hesitate or ask any questions. The pilots had all gone down to the Mess for tea. I was outwardly calm but inwardly cold, shivering all over, yet clear and absolutely determined now.

I looked around dispersal, nobody seemed to be taking much notice, so I started up and taxied out, fast, to the runway. Being strapped in felt queer. As I turned into wind I saw people running out from dispersal waving their arms. I looked F/S Ratcliffe full in the face as he gave the familiar signal "Switch Off" and then pushed the throttle forward as the tail came up, wide open through the gate. I did not look at my Air Speed Indicator and tried to pull her off too soon – at a Pisser speed – which caused the aeroplane to lurch into the air and sink back, drifting badly, but she came off and went up in a steep climb at just about stalling speed; 'hanging from propeller', as they say.

The tail was buffeting; I pushed the stick forward and she flicked down too far so that it was like a switch back. I could not help it, the pilot before me had left the tail trim right back and I hadn't known to check it, and also, things happened so much more than in the Pisser and she was so much more sensitive than my control. But the engine power saved me and I came to at about 1,000 feet, trimmed her, put my legs up, closed the hood, and pulled the throttle and prop control back to about 2,400 rpm at plus 4 pounds per square inch of boost. It was a horrible take off. Thus it was some time before I collected myself. I had hardly noticed where I had been going, just out to sea to the North and, moreover, the speed at which I was travelling, over 200 miles per hour, was beyond my sense of values. The weather here was bad, I had not reckoned with low cloud but already I was in the cloud-base at 3,000 feet. I could not get the map folded in the right place and when I did I could only see the coast line occasionally and could not recognise it; it was enemy territory. I dared not go near for fear of being shot at. And I still could not get used to the sensitive Spitfire.

I was alone and weaving all the time because I was afraid of being bounced if there were any Huns about. I could not find the flying instruments, altimeter and air speed indicator, at a glance. An emotional reaction set in, and with it, doubt, fear, ludicrous thoughts of home and security. I felt a despairing loneliness, as if I was already dead. I was near hysteria in the cockpit, which would have killed me.

But also there was a dispassionate interest in how the aeroplane I knew so well on the ground flew and I began to try things out – turns, dives, climbs, switched the reflector sight on, then turned it off again because it distracted my vision. I put the guns at fire and then diving at the sea fired off a few rounds. It felt just like I expected, the cannons shuddering and a little blue smoke.

Finally, still making my way north, with the coast line just in sight, and occasionally going through an odd cloud on the Artificial Horizon Compass, I throttled back, put my flaps down and practised gliding at abut 90 miles per hour, losing height. The Spit behaved much more like my old Pisser at this speed. Thus an exhilaration came over me and fought back the hysteria. A greatness, I was living as I had never lived efore – and I trust never will again. I was absorbed and lost in a complete singleness beyond this world. I was flying.

That singleness of mind carried me through till my feet were on the ground again.

I relocated my position from an unmistakeable landmark on the map. A great rock (Mt Arceo) which juts out south of the Pontine Marshes, which reassured me that I was not north of Rome by this time. There were one or two ships below me and I came down nearer to them, taking the line of their wake and waggling my wings at them in a friendly fashion. A few more minutes and I saw the beach-head, the ships standing off, the town of Anzio, and then, clearly, the Nettuno landing strip along the beach just below the town. Some bombers in formation startled me by flying overhead and there were odd flashes from the ground flak away to the east, a squadron of Spits on patrol above.

I kept well clear of the ships knowing how trigger conscious the Navy are and came down as low as I dared over the strip, flying up and down it once or twice, looking at it carefully. There was another Spit doing the same. There were lots of wrecks all over the aerodrome but the strip itself looked clear, so I climbed up again to 1,000 feet as per Tom's training, turned onto the down leg. Freddie had said it was only possible to land north to south, so the strip being torn up at the south end, throttled right back (I didn't touch it again, nor could have), put my legs down and with one eye on the strip and the other on the Air Speed Indicator, started to glide in. About 95 miles per hour, the tail started buffeting, so I remembered to put the flaps down (!) and kept the speed at a steady 90 on the stick, coming round in a wide sweep, looking over the port wing. I came over the boundary line at about the right height but too far round and, therefore, had to drop the starboard wing at the last moment to line up onto the strip. This slight weave though, helped me see. The ground came rushing up to meet me and at what seemed to me the last moment I pulled the stick back; the huge nose of the aircraft came up and obscured my vision completely.

There was nothing more to do. She bounced once then seemed to settle down, then started swinging off to the right. I felt the swing, still could not see, and although I jammed on full left rudder and braked I was sure the legs were about to collapse so violent was it, but they didn't and I pulled up, still on the strip, with a good 50 yards to spare before the torn up part, and taxied off. I jumped out of the cockpit and looked at the aeroplane with sheer surprise. My God, I'd done it.

I forgot; just after touching down, I saw another Spit pass over my head with flaps and legs down. It must have been the one I saw on the circuit, who came in the other way. Luckily, he saw me and went round again – indeed I don't think he ever did come in – for nothing on earth would have stopped me putting that aircraft down on that first approach; I was going to get down, crash or no crash, no doubt, nor fear, nor hesitation, and I could not have gone round again; that's all there was to it. That the aircraft wasn't damaged surprised me too but I had got to Nettuno.

The other Spit may have been flown by Group Captain Duncan Smith who had taken off to find me if he could and order me back to the Gela coast and to 'bale out'. But I had no radio and he lost me in the cloud. Then he correctly guessed that I would be making for Anzio and so covered my landing there. I do not know this for sure but it has been said that he landed too and had a chat with me to ensure that I would not try and fly back. I do not remember this conversation myself but G/Captain Duncan Smith was a great Commander and I do know that he did his best to save me from myself.

Thus, after six hours always dual on a Moth, of which Tom logged 1hr 50min as real training, I flew my first solo in a Spitfire! Also I had to beat bad weather, find my way to a strange aerodrome and avoid enemy action. But I wasn't finished by any means.

There was no one about on the 'drome, many crashed or wrecked aeroplanes of all sorts, and at the north end, one or two Spits parked. Half-way up the strip, standing almost on the strip and with, as Freddy had said, a Spit on which a shell had landed next to it, was JU-A. It looked intact, although some of the plugs were missing. No sign of Bamby. I walked over to a building at the top and found a couple of Yank pilots who were about to take off.

They had been delayed by unserviceability from getting away with the rest of 307 'F' Squadron aircraft who had gone at noon. They said that a British pilot had flown out on the last DC3 that afternoon and that the Hun had been shelling the 'drome intermittently all day. So Bamby being accounted for and it seeming fairly quiet, apart from the perpetual booming of guns, which never stopped in the beach-head while I was there, I went to work on 'A'.

I had taken the cowlings off, reviewed the job, inspected the petrol filter and was changing the plugs, which it needed, with those from a crash of '43's' nearby which were good, when, very suddenly, there came the familiar old scream of dive bombers and I dived for the deck while merry hell broke loose. 109's or 190's were bombing the beach closely, for I felt the bombs bursting but saw none it the 'drome and at the same time, every gun on the land and on the ships opened up. I crawled under the engine to avoid falling shrapnel. It was all over as quickly as it started except that the ships went on firing off odd rounds aimlessly. A patrol of Spits streamed off to the East and, of course, the big guns went on booming and the machine guns rat-tat-tatting. I started work again but I could not concentrate, my hands were shaking so much I couldn't find the correct threads to screw plugs in.

About ten minutes later, I looked up to see a Spit on the circuit streaming glycol. I said to myself, "Good show, here comes a pilot to take 'U' back". He put his legs down, but I thought he hadn't enough height to make the strip, then he found a few more engine revolutions which lasted just long enough before oil streamed out all over the kite and the engine seized. He put his legs up again, which made me swear because he might spoil the strip, but he could not see and belly-landed with a nasty crunch about one third way up the strip. The kite had 'HN' written on the side so I knew it was one of our Wing and when I got to him it was "Screw" Rivett of 93 Squadron, an old acquaintance. He was radioing to others of the squadron above to tell them he was OK and I told him to tell them that I had a fly-back ready for him, which he did. Then a dialogue something like this took place; we were both shaken remember:

"What the bleeding hell are you doing here Spanner?"

"Never mind that, blast you", I said, "there's a 'V' of III's here and its bloody hot round this joint so the sooner you get out the better. Take it back and tell them I'm OK."

"What's wrong with it?" he said, "will you give me your word it's serviceable?"

"Of course the bastard thing's serviceable, I've just flown it up here!" I replied somewhat illogically, then, "and tell them I'm not going to fly anything back myself."

As he was getting strapped in he said, "I don't think there's enough runway left to get off over my prang."

I was frantic to get him away and started madly swearing at him again for just then the ack-ack opened up again but before he had time to get out of the cockpit the two IX's of the 307th took off, easily clearing his wreck, and this reassured him together with our mutual opinion that this was neither the time nor the place to hang around. So he taxied off up the strip and I ran as fast as I could for a slit trench. The roar of old U's engine as he came down the runway on take off, eclipsed the banging guns and bombs and the scream of aerobatics. He pulled her over the wreck and soon became a black speck in the gathering dusk. Just then a lonely jeep came across the 'drome and I hailed it.

"I'm stuck here, can you fix me up, for the night possibly?"

It turned out to be the Radio Officer of the 307th. He took me off the strip and about two miles inland past a great tented hospital, to a high bank of earth, into the south-west side of which a few tents nestled. There I met my old pal, Jim Ivors, engineer of the US 307th, whom I had first met at Biggin Hill and we had run along parallel ever since. He said that his aircraft evacuated that morning because it was impossible to operate within range of the German artillery; and that the ground crews were still here but, after the last two days would not go on the 'drome but he hoped to get two more of his squadron's and our 'A', on which he knew what was needed, away if and when the shelling lessened. He said they had had three weeks of it and were all pretty tired. He was greatly amused at me coming up there in a Spit and I think glad to see someone he knew from the outside world. He told me that there had been a different British pilot in the bed in which I was to sleep for the last four nights, all force landed, and I told him of our plug and water troubles. He was worried abut his men. We discussed the old enthusiastic days of Souk el Arba, and the different outlook now. That morning he had asked for volunteers to work on our 'A' and no one had volunteered I told him it was just the same with our blokes. It was just endurance now, steady practised efficient work with little inspiration, men browned off, waiting only for the end of it all.

As we were talking in the dimly lit tent, round a warm wood stove, an '88' was droning about overhead, the everlasting gun fire was banging away. We were all wearing tin hats. The odd bombs dropped but must have been far away. It was then I heard my first shell 'Wailing Winnie' as they called it, a kind of whirring whine and a pop as it exploded behind us. How I appreciated that bank then; nothing but a Howitzer could hit us and even then the tent was extended right under the bank on one side to make a sort of dug-out.

The noise and shaking of the ground went on all night and I could not sleep very much.

Next morning, after waiting till, as Jim said, "the milk train had gone through", that is to say the regular dawn dive-bombing of the strip was over, we went back there. We found that the operations shed had received a direct hit from a shell in the night and standing beside the ruins was F/Lt Richardson – another old acquaintance – flight commander of '93'. He also had crash landed on the strip that morning and said he would be only too glad to fly 'A' back when I had got it ready, his own aircraft being bent. Jim loaned me some tools and offered any help but I said that Richy and I could do everything until it came to the run up test when we should need some men to hold the tail down.

I forgot, before breakfast up at the tent, we saw a Lightning shot down. It was a marvellous sight, right overhead. We watched it from the beginning at 15,000 feet approximately, ending up in the town of Anzio. This Lightning was weaving about evidently with about three, what looked like, Spitfires on his tail, one after the other, all flashing in the sun. He was in a steep turn when one engine began streaming black smoke, then a red blob of fire growing. Suddenly a parachute appeared in the blue sky, hanging like a little tiny cloud but very white and sharply outlined.

The Spits broke away and one of them circled the parachutist before flying off south. Meanwhile the Lightning was going down in a steep spin, flaming and leaving a trail of smoke. The tail came clean off and fell vertically apart from the rest. (This happened after the pilot baled out – although there is, in Lightnings, a way of blowing off the tail before baling out, as the tail often hits the falling pilot otherwise. Maybe the pilot tried to blow it off in this case without immediate success).

The mass of the aircraft fell right in the middle of the little town, a wing coming off just before it hit and burst into a red and black explosion among the houses. The pilot did not seem to be coming down at all but, eventually, the parachute got larger and he landed in the sea about ten minutes later. I heard when I got back to Lago that some of our boys while on patrol had been told by the Controller to go for this Lightning; it might have been a German PRU (Photo reconnaissance plane) in disguise but the Yanks I was with were a bit disgruntled about it at the time.

To continue . . . .

As I was saying, Richy and I then went out onto the open strip. He was helping me do the plug change when some more shells came whirring over and exploded. We ran as fast as we could to a dug-out on the beach about fifty yards away. But every time we came out and went back to work another couple came over making us duck and run until, as we had only got the inlet plugs to finish and as only one person could do any work, Richy stayed in the trench while I was perched up on top of the Spit's nose, regardless. The shelling went on intermittently all morning. I had been told that if you heard the noise of one, it had missed you, which didn't seem to be much encouragement.

I emptied some spark plugs out of my cap and put it on my head for a little comfort, but once again I couldn't concentrate on the work. It was strange being the only person in sight, on the top of a Spit standing on that open airfield littered with

wrecks, in a frightfully exposed position. I thought of what
Mother would say if she saw me, and of the sunlit peace of our
aerodrome among the trees of Lago. But I was absolutely
determined to get that aircraft away; never been so fixed of
purpose before in my life, a sort of cold anger, and I noticed
that the shells were falling into the sea between us and some
ships. They were probably trying to hit the ships and couldn't
quite reach them, I hoped. So by a sort of conscious disregard
of everything else going on around me, I worked on, until the
last plug was in and the last lead connected.

When I first inspected 'A' after I had arrived, there was no
sign of any damage to it as a result of the shelling although the
kite next door to it had been hit badly, but when I looked it
over before Richy took off, there was one exhaust pipe on the
engine chipped and bent where a bit of shrapnel must have
hit it. I don't know when that happened, must have been
during the night or when Richy and I were in the dug-out,
though I told the flight crew of the aircraft back at Lago, that
it happened while I was working on it!

With Jim, Richy and a couple of Yanks on the tail, I
ground-tested the kite thoroughly. Took it up to 18 lbs/square
inch boost to make sure Richy could get off the torn up and
littered strip. Everything was alright except that it had a drop
on the port mag. pronounced. I must have missed one of the
exhaust plugs, which I confirmed to be so back at the base,
but I told Richy that in spite of that she'd be OK to get him
home, and neither of us wanted to start looking for a duff plug
at that juncture. Richy said he'd take my word for its being
good enough, so we strapped him in and off he went, while
my heart beat violently till he was out of sight.

It was all very well for me to be taking risks, I had a lot at stake, and above all I had to get that kite back if I was to survive the mud-stirring which Richy had said was already going on about my unorthodox means of travel, but old Richy could just as well have hurried off onto a ship after he crashed, or laid low until some air transport came in to be taken back, but that pilot got his hands dirty, stood by under shell fire and then risked his neck to fly a kite back for me; I've got a lot of time for F/Lt Richardson of '93' Squadron.

Meanwhile, an American Fairchild 4-seater had come in and was parked at the end of the strip behind the operations rubble. He was from the 31st Group. I had tried to borrow it myself earlier in the week and he was carrying despatches. I fixed up with the pilot to take me back when he went. There was only room for one passenger and there was another claimant, an American, but the matter was settled by the timely arrival, at high speed, in a jeep, of two tin-hatted Yank MP's from somewhere, to put me under immediate close arrest – this by radio from Lago. They didn't know what to do with me once they had got me, and I wouldn't come off the aerodrome because there was more work to do there on two more of '324' Wing's kites, so a neat arrangement was made whereby they made the pilot of the Fairchild my escort to take me back to my evermore wrathful Group Captain. They then tore off again as fast as they had come.

During the course of this, one or two other interesting happenings are worth noting. First of all, earlier on, another 'III' Squadron kite had landed; it was Bill Young in 'Y', who while on patrol had found petrol in the bottom of his cockpit, increasing, and therefore had force-landed on the strip. He was carrying a jettison tank and it was caused by what it usually is – the connection on the belly leaking – so I just dropped the tank, showed him the leak had stopped and pushed him off again without further ado. This slow petrol leak is not dangerous and he could perfectly well have gone home with it had not the Nettuno strip been there.

After that I saw from a ringside seat, the ditching of a Fortress. It must have been hit by Hun flak on one of the almost continual bombing sorties over the lines, for it came very low over the strip twice, with two engines stopped and dropping things – films, maps, etc. – then made a wide circle out to sea, throttled back and glided down onto the sea right between two ships. As it ditched, a great spume of sea-spray was sent up – a marvellous sight, the huge bomber flying onto the sea, and it was still floating ten minutes later when I looked again. I was glad he didn't try to crash on the strip which might have made it impossible for Richy to take off but I never heard the story of it, nor saw any of the crew get out. Next we had a Mitchell or Marauder, I forget which, having been shot up, try to land on the strip on one leg. Neither the nose leg nor the starboard main leg was down. He came in very fast and as the mainplanes lost lift speed he overshot the end of the strip, the right wing dropped, causing a violent swing to starboard and ended up, properly pranged, off the end of the strip facing out to sea.

Then, just before Richy took off, a Spit landed, 'FT' of 43 Squadron, and I waved him in to where my tools were as Richy taxied out. I thought I might put a sign up, "Farish School of Flying – ITW, FTS, OTU Aircraft Repairs done while you wait". It was an Australian pilot and his engine had cut, then picked up again and was running alright now. The fuel filters, after a lot of sleight of hand to get at them, were clean enough, but it was the same old trouble, deposit on the plugs.

While I was on Nettuno I had a walk round some of the Spits pranged there. Very many of them had this plug trouble, some frightful, and obviously the cause of all these mysterious engine failures that the Wing had been having. But 'FT's' plugs were not very bad and so, ascertaining that she had only cut after he had used high boost chasing Huns, I ran it up, testing ignition, then told him she'd be OK to go back, only not to use more than plus 4. This he did, taking off with an enormous run the whole length of the strip at plus 4, which was taking me too literally, and got back safely.

Then, having nothing more to do, I went across to the Fairchild pilot, who was still waiting for the mail bag, and we sat looking out from our foxhole smoking and talking.

I saw a sight I had never seen before although the boys used to shoot lines at me about it happening at Salerno, that of our own bombers bombing. A dozen or more Mitchells, or Bostons, would come sweeping in from out to sea, in tight formation, not very high, and fly steadily west into the Hun flak, which came up at them in masses as soon as they were in range. They never seemed to alter course much, but rather fly right through all the bursting black puffs and then with their noses slightly down, run fast over the target, turn, still in formation and fly off south, out to sea again, leaving behind them great clouds of dirt hanging in the air over the enemy lines where the bombs had landed.

It looked as if nothing could survive the terrible pattern of chaos as the bombs burst, yet the ack-ack never faltered and the big guns went on booming all the time. And then another formation would come in – all morning, squadron after squadron of bombers sailed majestically overhead, the dust hung over the battle front and the noise went on. We also saw the process going on the other way round. FW 190's and ME 109's bombing us, which made me one up on the Salerno boys. This was always marked by the staccato objections of machine gun fire from the ships close by, that above the increase in noise, that noise of explosions which seemed never to have stopped since I landed on the beach-head the day before; an eternity of bangs.

While we were waiting thus, I was telling the pilot of my experiences, and of what it had been like here for the last twenty-four hours, until finally he said, "Oh, to hell with that mail, let's get out of here, the next ship can bring it along". I heartily endorsed that opinion and we climbed into the Fairchild, I praying to myself for fear it would not start. I had got away with so much, could my luck hold just a little bit longer? Something seemed bound to go wrong. It started; we took off from the deserted aerodrome of wrecked planes, and flew out to sea, then southward. As we passed by a warship, a cruiser I think, we saw a big gun fire at us, the flame licked the lips of the gun-barrel. It must have been a warning shot not to come so close, but to me it was a parting shot. I prayed harder, never was a dispatch aeroplane so slow, and so defenceless, and so difficult to see from above and behind, as that Fairchild, and I did not stop praying until it landed me safe and sound among the trees and sun and peace of Lago.

Hospital again. But this time in the most odd circumstances; yesterday they psycho-analysed me and today they are going to X-ray my head. In fact, there is nothing wrong with my sanity, any more than there usually is, but these formalities, as they put it, are a polite way of keeping me in open arrest for – "In that by any act caused damage or was liable to cause damage to one of his Majesty's aircraft", or something like that. And this is how it all came about.

While I was still in hospital, two experts from Rolls Royce Derby arrived, not ordinary field Rolls Royce representatives but chosen because they had experience of both the development and operation of the Merlin 66 in England, and for two days investigated and correctly diagnosed the real problem. It turned out that the silicone deposits on the spark plugs which had so worried me were actually only a symptom of something more serious, which was that traces of water were getting into the petrol supply.

The bowsers from which the petrol was delivered to the aircraft were found to contain some water, but after this water had been drained out, more was found in the bowsers after they themselves had been re-fuelled from the main storage supply. So the trouble was really coming from the latter. Extra precautions to ensure a really clean main supply were immediately taken and then with clean bowsers being checked every day the silicone deposits on the spark plugs disappeared and the engines ran smoothly throughout their range so that there was no more trouble. Obviously I should have gone to W/C Woodbury for top level help long before my extraordinary flight drew such dramatic attention to our problems.

It is ironic but more than possible that I myself may have fixed the general problem by my emphasis to the flight crews on the need for exceptionally clean and frequently drained bowsers, although of course, I did not know this at the time. In my opinion now the Merlin 66 engines which we had pioneered overseas were more sensitive to traces of water being in the petrol supply than the Merlin 61's in the Spit IX's. This may well have been fixed by Rolls Royce later, by finer filter screens for instance. I never had the opportunity to talk with the Rolls Royce development men myself but would clearly have liked to have done so.

Endnotes to Diaries

Containing additional information for the period up to the end of the campaign in Sicily – August 1943

by Michael McCaul

(Numbers refer to Part 3, The Diaries)

1.) In June 1942, Squadron Leader R W 'Bobby' Oxspring DFC, assumed command of 72 (Basutoland) Squadron at Biggin Hill, an 11 Group station, and from where the squadron was involved in cross-channel operations as part of the Kenley Wing, led by W/Cmr 'Jamie' Rankin.

On 15 July, 72 Squadron received orders to prepare to move, with their Spitfire VBs to Morpeth, north of Newcastle. This transfer to 13 Group came as an unpleasant shock to the squadron. In the first place, it dashed such hopes as there had been of converting to Spitfire IXs with their Merlin 61 engines, and which the CO and both the then Flight commanders had flown at Biggin Hill and had found very much to their liking. Secondly, the only thing known about Morpeth, other than that it was a wartime hutted camp, was that it was not far from Ashington, a mining village where the squadron had made so many friends during its time at Acklington in August 1940.

The Squadron's last operation from Biggin Hill was on 1 August; a sweep to Bruges and Flushing. Earlier, on 25 July, the squadron had been in action over Northern France against FW 190s and in effect demonstrated to 'Bobby' Oxspring what a good squadron he had taken over.

The squadron's aircraft reached Morpeth on 4 August, after being grounded on account of bad weather at Duxford. On 12 August, the squadron moved again – this time to RAF Station Ayr. It was at Ayr that the squadron was told that it had been selected for deployment overseas and that this would involve a significant increase in establishment to enable the squadron to operate as a mobile and self-sufficient unit in the field. It was at Ayr, as a nineteen year old volunteer for service overseas, I had the good fortune to join 72 Squadron, as an LAC Clerk, from RAF Records at Ruislip.

2.)   While at Ayr, some Squadron aircraft were detached to Drem, from where Bobby Oxspring led a joint 72/222 Squadron force to join in the air operations undertaken in support of the ill-fated Dieppe raid on 19 August.

It was also at Ayr that some squadron aircraft took part in military exercises in the West of Scotland, known as Dryshod, which were in fact rehearsals for the eventual landings in TORCH.

At Ayr, there were many new arrivals, including an RAF Regiment contingent, and the new establishment just exceeded 300, all ranks. There were also some departures, some on medical grounds, as well as a number of well merited promotions of existing members of the ground staff, some of whom had been with '72' since 1939. New pilots were selected (with care) by the CO and for the first time the Squadron acquired not only a Cypher Officer (Van der Veen), but also an Intelligence Officer (Sims). The indispensable Squadron Adjutant, 'Tiny' Le Petit, was promoted to Flight Lieutenant; the Squadron Medical Officer was a Dubliner –

Paddy Griffin. Later, while at Ouston, the vacant Engineer Officer post was filled by Flying Officer Gregory Farish of 222 Squadron, at Drem. It will be recalled that '72' had been detached to Drem in August, and it may well have been more than co-incidence that Farish came to join our Squadron in October.

On 26 September, the squadron moved on to Ouston, a 13 Group Station near Newcastle, and where preparations for service overseas began in earnest. Inoculations, physical training, cross-country running, weapon training (including an introduction to the Sten gun), and packing of equipment, occupied most of our time, but there were also opportunities to sample the social life of Newcastle, and to walk miles across the moors to our favourite pub at Long Horsley. The squadron handed over their aircraft on 12 October; some went to the US Army Air Force units already in residence at Ouston. By this time the Squadron had acquired a low threshold of boredom which in the absence of any leave, was relieved only in the third week of October when all but two of the pilots (who came with us) made their discreet departures to unannounced destinations, but which appeared to be not far from the Mersey!

In the absence of the CO, Tiny Le Petit decided on 2 November to grant some short leaves (4 days) to those who had not any embarkation leave. I was one of the lucky ones, and reached home on 3 November. But at 0630 hours on 5 November, the village policeman called to inform my mother that "he is to return immediately, repeat immediately" to Ouston. Some 45 minutes later I was aboard the only early morning bus to Berkhamsted and was at Kings Cross to catch the 1000 hours departure for Newcastle. Everyone on the train was agog with the 8th Army's great victory at El Alamein, news of which had reached London the previous evening. I said nothing, but reflected – with relief – that clearly we would not be wanted in the North African desert!

Back at Ouston, all was anti-climax, and apart from being confined to camp, nothing really happened until 7 November (Saturday) when we were told of our departure, "in the morning". And thus it was that at about 0430 hours we lined up dressed in khaki battle dress, carrying full packs, full ammunition pouches, steel helmets, and a Sten gun apiece, and were taken to Newcastle station, where we boarded a troop train and left for an undisclosed destination.

The fog and dirty windows made it impossible to see where we were going and speculation was rife. My recollection is that the first station that we were able to identify was Ashton-under-Lyme; along the route which then led us to the Liverpool docks, we saw many people out walking to church.

At the docks, we found the MV Staffordshire waiting for us, along with Greggs Farish, and his advance party. It was from him that we first received the 'gen' that there had been landings of Anglo/American troops in French North Africa earlier in the day. Now, at last, we knew where we were going!

3.) Both on and around the 'Staffordshire' we found ourselves heavily outnumbered by the military, who were taken aback by our khaki battledress and our Sten guns. One member of our RAF Regiment 'flight' was taken aboard as a prisoner since only two days previously he had been awarded twenty seven days detention for indiscretions of a security nature on the telephone, which had been reported by the Civil Censor. As there were no cells on board, he was released, but another member of the squadron who had earlier received a similar punishment from the Station Commander at Ouston had been less fortunate; in fact he served his twenty seven days at Sowerby Bridge. Twenty seven days had been awarded in each case rather than the maximum punishment of twenty eight days available to the Station Commander; the lesser sentence attracted no remission! Years later (and as a colleague) I taxed that

Station Commander about his use of this ruse, but he affected to have no recollection of such matters!

4.) We left the Mersey on the afternoon of 12 November, and while we went down river the ship's anti-aircraft guns were tested, without notice, and many of us smelt 'cordite' for the first time. The next morning we found ourselves moving up the Clyde past familiar places such as Ayr and Arran, before passing into the heavily protected anchorage at Gourock and joining several other large transports.

5.) On board there were gunners, mapmakers (who worked in a locked cabin throughout the voyage) and Provost staff in plenty. Like us the soldiery found nothing to enthuse about in the sardine-like accommodation provided on the troop decks.

6.) We sailed at 1600 hours on Saturday, 14 November as a member of convoy KMF/3. We had our last sight of land on Sunday morning, when for the first time we were able to appreciate the size of our convoy and the number of naval escorts. We noted that we were on the port flank of the convoy and learned from one of the ship's (Army – 6 Armoured Division) gunners that we had been so placed to ensure full use of the Staffordshire's firepower, which was unusually powerful for a merchant ship of her size.

On the second day out, rough weather intervened and predictably caused much discomfort on the troop decks which, after dark, were the only places where smoking was permitted. The combination of tobacco smoke and people being sick led me to opt to sleep on the open deck, under a lifeboat, for the rest of the trip. I was therefore well placed to head the queue for tea from the ship's canteen at 6.30 am; an orderly queue was ensured by the presence of a 'Red Cap' and with one of whom, Cpl. Bowes (a Yorkshireman but with no cricketing background!), I had some pleasant chats. I actually spotted the same Corporal, covered with dust, on point duty directing traffic as we passed by in May 1943 on our way from Souk el Khemis to a new camp at Mateur; we gave him a cheer as we recognised him and he waved back.

7.)   We passed Gibraltar on the evening of 20 November, a day on which we saw one of our escorts drop a number of depth charges; rumour had it that a U-Boat had been sunk but scrutiny of official records does not confirm this. On 21 November, we had a distant glimpse of the Balearics before turning south for the run into Algiers. Near sunset there was some heavy AA fire on the other side of the convoy at enemy reconnaissance aircraft. Our last supper on board was of boiled eggs and salt pork; the sea was dead calm but during the night, and whether on account of the food or of nervous tension, I was 'sick as a dog'. However, we all woke on Sunday 22 November to a hazy view of the bay of Algiers and resigned ourselves to a long wait. But in fact, we were called in after what seemed only a short wait, and on our way we exchanged greetings with the crews of some of the rust-marked destroyers which had escorted us safely to Algiers from the Clyde.

8.)   Eventually we marched off in full kit to a disused warehouse where we were to stay the night during which there was a tremendous barrage of AA fire at a number of German and Italian raiders, including one which torpedoed a ship which, it transpired, was waiting to unload hundreds of bags of mail addressed to APO 9225, and as a result thousands of men already in North Africa, as well as those on the convoy, were without mail for weeks.

9.)   Next day, our drivers went off with Greggs Farish, but the rest of us moved to the beach at Hussein Dey, which was not only used for horse racing, but also to drain rainwater into the sea from the higher ground. We were issued with two-man American fly tents but as we put them up, so it started to rain in earnest; it was not long before the beach became a lake and most of our kit began to float around. Our next move was to a deserted Girl's school on the higher ground, where we dried out and stayed until Friday 27 November when we went down to the docks, in lorries, to await some kind of sea transport to move us eastwards towards Tunisia, where our pilots were already in action at Souk el Arba. I have an indelible memory of watching the arrival that morning in Algiers of HMS Sirius, a five-inch cruiser, said to have been in action at sea the previous night. In any event, within only a few minutes of docking, there were countless parties of sailors at work on deck, and not long afterwards a small Royal Marine band (with white helmets) emerged to play on the forecastle. For me, it was a memorable moment and made me feel then as proud of being British as I am today.

10.)   Eventually, we were told to board HMS Bicester, a Hunt class destroyer, which had also been in action the night before, and in which we were conveyed to Phillipeville overnight. The loquacious and good natured Cockney leading hand, whose mess deck we were invading, left us in no doubt that the trip would be no 'picnic'. He was right, but nevertheless we enjoyed the experience rather more than anything else that happened in the ensuing seven days, in which, frustratingly, we were to travel by train no more than 200 miles from Phillipeville to Souk el Arba, via Souk Ahras. But even this crawl had its moments; on the Sunday morning, one of the many stops made (for no apparent reason) was close to a British Army unit, whose Chaplain was about to celebrate Communion, using the back of a 15 cwt truck as an altar. We were invited to attend, which we did, while keeping an eye on our unpredictable train. From all around, droves of white-clad Arabs suddenly appeared to watch this ritual – in respectful silence.

On the journey from Souk Ahras we found ourselves sharing the train with a company of the Parachute Brigade, and with a French African (some said Senegalese) cavalry unit, horses and all. One of our stops lasted a whole day, with our train half in and half outside a tunnel. The horses were inside the tunnel, from which large quantities of steaming horse-dung were removed to be dumped on the side of the track near us! The Paras allowed none of this to deflect them from duty; indeed during such stops they put up a table, with green baize top, on the side of the track and set about holding some formal enquiry, which involved much shouting by their ramrod of a Sergeant Major, as witnesses were marshalled for interrogation. We were mightily impressed by the discipline displayed. All sorts of reasons, none of which flattered the French, were adduced for the appalling delay, but eventually on 5 December, having got as far as the frontier post of Ghademou, we positively dashed down the straight to Souk el Arba; the railway rain in parallel with the road which, we discovered, was already known as 'Messerschmidt' alley.

11.)   We were delighted to reach Souk el Arba at 'tea time' on 5 December, not least for the reason that we had had no news of our pilots since leaving Algiers on 27 November, although some of the news we had heard about British troops having penetrated to within twenty miles of Tunis, made us wonder why we had come at all. We duly met up with the pilots and with the fitters and drivers who had formed the advance guard led by Greggs Farish. In particular we were sorry to hear of the deaths in action of Sgts Mottram and Browne, as well as of Pilot Officer Johnnie Lowe.

The next two days were hectic and in addition to putting up tents, digging slit trenches and filling up sand-bags, there was a need to erect the camouflaged awnings (using instructions which were not at all helpful!) around the brand new purpose-built mobile office which had come out all the way from the UK. We also experienced enemy raids for the first time; sometimes bombs, sometimes machine-gun fire, but with practically no warning. On 7 December, my 20th Birthday, I was on my way to attend to a map in the 'Dispersal' tent when the strip was strafed by FW 190s. I dived for cover into the tent, where at least I could not be seen!

So nearly seven weeks after the pilots had left us at Ouston, the Squadron was reunited at Souk el Arba, and from this point onwards, Greggs Farish's own diaries tell the rest of the story aided by a number of unique photographs which he himself took at the time.

12.)   It has to be said that the decision to split the Squadron and to move those deemed to be 'non-essential' at Souk el Arba to a hillside olive grove near Ghademou was not at all popular with the airmen, or indeed conducive of good morale. There were of course valid reasons for the move, although in terms of exposure to enemy action, there was no more vulnerable spot than the Souk el Arba–Ghademou 'straight', along which everyone had to move.

Nor was Ghademou exactly a health resort; for example, one of our two 'redundant' photographers (our Spitfires carried no cameras) rusticated to Ghademou, had the misfortune to be stung by a scorpion while sleeping on his groundsheet. He was fortunate in that the Squadron MO lost no time in acquiring the necessary antidote from French Medical sources in Algiers; this photographer – whose name escapes me, although it began with an 'A', is in fact the third man in photograph…

While Ghademou was certainly a place where the pilots could take a short break and find it possible to relax amongst the olive trees, there were no regrets when in late January, the squadron was once again reunited and 're-housed' at Souk el Khemis.

13.)   The actual date of the raid on Chouigui, in which Wing Commander Malcolm earned his posthumous Victoria Cross was 4 December 1942.

14.)   The date of 152 Squadron's unfortunate experience at Medjez-el-Bab was 5 December 1942. '152' did, in fact, return to Soul el Khemis as part of 322 Wing and designated as a fighter bomber squadron. (Regarding 72's experience in 1940, 72, between 29 September and 13 October 1940 lost five (Officer) pilots, and some nine aircraft before being withdrawn to Leconfield; having been at Biggin Hill since 1 September 1940.)

15.)   I spent Christmas Day on the road to Ghademou, acting as a 'look-out' in the back of a three-tonner. For some reason we were directed off the road for a time, and in pouring rain three of us had our Christmas dinner off some cold 'M & V', and cold Syrup pudding. No beer, nor indeed much else, at Ghademou!

16.)   I think that there must have been more than one case of a Fitter being taken on an involuntary circuit while clinging onto the tail of 'his' Spitfire. I recall seeing this happen at Souk el Arba soon after our arrival there; the story was that the unfortunate airman involved had to be invalided home.

17.)   111 Squadron began to use the newly laid strip at Souk el Khemis on 30 December; '72' moved in to 'Euston' as one of the new strips being laid there was known, on 15 January 1943.

18.)   Squadron pilots left for Gibraltar on 1 February and, flying their new IXs, returned to Souk el Khemis on 25 February 1943, a day of rain, low cloud and thunder storms. It had not been too wet, however, to prevent a football match – 'Admin v. Flights' – being played. Somehow 'Admin' won and I scored a goal. The game was remarkable not only because I was 'marked' (in more ways than one!) by Aircraftsman Cullis, cousin of the great Stan Cullis, captain of England, but more seriously for the fact that just after our game had ended, one of the returning Spitfire IXs crashed and the pilot, Sgt Passmore was killed. It was a sad occasion; 'Tiny' Le Petit organised the funeral and had a photograph taken for the next of kin. Some months later a letter of complaint from an MP was received about an 'inappropriate inscription' on the cross made in the squadron.

19.) 'Chas' Charnock did indeed have a bottle of whisky in his hand at Ghademou on New Year's Eve, which he shared with some airmen including myself, who had not previously tasted the stuff. The next day he was to return to Souk el Arba ostensibly to 'test his nerve' as a pilot, but as he did not stay on there for more than a day or so, we assumed that in fact he had failed his test; presumably, however, he left after it had been found that his medical clearance to fly again was not genuine.

There was an amusing incident later at Souk el Khemis when a posse of Army Provost staff turned up to arrest 'Chas' as an absentee from the Army hospital (?Souk Ahras) from which he had discharged himself in December after his third crash landing. What the Provost did not know was that immediately after leaving the hospital, he had 'flagged' down an RAF staff car on the road outside and found that its occupant (an Air Commodore) had been a contemporary of 'Chas' at Cranwell and was only too glad to offer 'Chas' a lift all the way 'home'.

My last news of 'Chas' was that he had fallen and broken a limb while going aboard a troopship in Algiers. For me it had been a privilege to read his log book; I particularly relished an entry "1/5th German destroyer sunk off Holland in 1942."

20.) It fell to me – an LAC – to keep an eye on those high value 'escape purses', in moisture-proof envelopes, to ensure that the seals remained intact. I will say no more than that this task caused me many headaches for how could I prove that I had not misappropriated the contents of the envelopes, from which 'Sovs' were said to have "just fallen out"?!

21.)   Presumably after the CO's briefing of Greggs Farish, Tiny Le Petit told me (evening of 25 March) that the CO wished me also to go down to Thelepte with the convoy. In fact I acted as map reader in the lorry driven by Cpl. Fletcher and in which the estimable F/Sgt Landon also travelled.

I recall a sticky moment at Le Kef where I sensed that someone had been interfering with the direction post; a wrong turning there might have taken us towards enemy territory. I guessed right and as dawn broke we were able to take a look at the abandoned tanks and guns in the Kasserine Pass.

Cpl 'Chick' Fowler who was seriously injured was a friend of mine and in fact, I had been with him only seconds before the mine went off. I had left him because I could not stand the stench from a long-dead donkey, near which the landmine had been placed.

At Thelepte, the US Army Air Force Officers were very kind and helpful after they had recovered from the surprise of meeting an LAC 'Intelligence Officer'; the food at Thelepte was 'absolutely fabulous'.

As a 'Spit IX' squadron, we had gone to Thelepte at the behest of our new masters at NATAF who by then had assumed control both of the Desert Air Force and of our own much smaller 'show' in 242 Group. Our purpose in going down to Thelepte on the morning of 26 March, was to provide 'top cover' for a US bombing mission to be made in support of General Patton's American troops in the Maknassy area. Bad visibility caused the mission to be cancelled but in morning sweeps over the Maknassy area, 72 Squadron destroyed two and damaged one of some fifteen enemy fighters poised to attack some American flown Spitfire VBs.

Aircraftsman Hitt, one of those most seriously injured by the land mine, did not rejoin the squadron after what was a lengthy stay in hospital, but found himself posted to a unit near Oran.

22.)   Nothing good comes to mind when recollecting our time at Mateur, to which we were hurried forward on 20 May from our reasonably comfortable quarters at Souk el Khemis, notwithstanding the fact that our aircraft were still to operate from La Sebala, near Tunis. The food at Mateur was both poor and in short supply. There was little shade and I remember particularly our lunches consisting of 'melted' corned beef competing on a plate with an awful American product called "Oleo-Margarine" (made and tasting of coconut oil) and the traditional Army biscuit, plus – as an occasional treat – the unspeakable 'Soya links'!

Mateur was also somewhat unhealthy – sand-fly fever was rife. We really felt out of things there too, particularly when we were told only at the last minute about a Victory parade at Carthage (we did not even know that 72's aircraft were to fly past), and the anticipated presence of Winston Churchill. We left Mateur at dawn in a 15 cwt truck, but got only as far as El Aouina airport on our way into Tunis, before being sidelined by the Military Police. We did not therefore reach Carthage in time to hear Winston speak, but at least we had a close-up of him alighting from his Avro York transport; he looked so pale.

The rest of the day was spent in Tunis where I was called upon to employ my French, and as a result of which we were invited into a French family residence. We later went down to form a queue for what we thought was a 'safe' water point. But it turned out to be a bonded warehouse, apparently spared in the Allied bombing of Tunis, and in which huge sealed vats of red wine had been found, as well as a supply of bottles. Just as miraculously, some Gurkha troops turned up and those splendid warriors needed little persuasion to use their kukris on the seals, which they did with relish and to tremendous effect, even though the wielder of the kukri had to stand on the shoulders of other Gurkhas to reach the seals; the scene would have gone well at a Royal Tournament!

Within minutes the warehouse was awash and we all went home with bottles of wine and wet feet.

On our way to the docks we had passed other queues, controlled by MPs, outside what were recognisable as brothels. I found this sight no more edifying than that which I had of an entry to be placed in the Officer's Confidential order book, mentioning the time at which an establishment for Officers would be opening its doors in Tunis on the same day.

As the diary indicates, there was little operational flying to be done at Mateur, after the aircraft had arrived from La Sebala, but one evening at the end of May, 'Sex' Gear was the leader of two aircraft off the Northern Tunisian coast, which at about 25,000 feet 'bounced' and shot down a lone German reconnaissance aircraft then described as an Me 210. However, post war research suggests that the aircraft almost certainly was a Me 410, a squadron of which had then recently been moved to Trapani in Sicily from Norway.

Before we left Mateur on 3 June, we were visited by a Base personnel officer anxious to prune out establishment of 'surplus bodies' and this involved saying goodbye to a number of men who were to remain in North Africa. Some were glad but most were sorry to leave the squadron.

While en route to Malta from Sfax (8/9 June) we passed close to the island of Djerba, and in the evening the Methodist padre (Squadron Leader Rooke) held a well attended service; he was a popular figure and maintained a somewhat higher profile among the airmen than his Church of England and Roman Catholic counterparts on 324 Wing.

Before leaving Souk el Khemis, all had been sorry to hear of the death after abdominal surgery, performed in an Army hospital, of Corporal Southwick of 'B' Flight. He was the only member of the groundstaff to be lost in Tunisia; the Engineer Officer wrote an appropriate letter of sympathy to his family in the Midlands.

The Squadron's standard of health at Souk el Khemis had been remarkably good, apart from those who suffered from gingivitis and other gum ailments induced by the Army biscuits. It had been feared that the Mejerda valley would prove to be a prolific source of malaria, and a stringent programme of prophylactic measures was introduced in mid-April: in particular an untried American product Atabrin (the British equivalent was Mepacrin) was to be taken at parade; slacks and long sleeves became de rigeur after dark. The morning after the first intake of Atabrin saw more than half the squadron quite unfit for duty; some men had turned quite yellow. We then were placed on 'half dose' and I do not recall any serious problems thereafter; it has been said that the only malaria case in the squadron in Tunisia involved the MO himself! In fact Sicily was to prove far more of a health hazard than Tunisia.

Living on a farm in proximity to Arab dwellings and where flies abounded, meant that particular attention had to be paid to our own sanitation and hygiene. Our 'sanitary' man was an 'elderly' airman remembered as Percy (?)Bolton, who earned every scrap of the extra sixpence per day that he received in 'sanitary' pay. There was also a risk of lice infestation and in addition to anti-typhus injections, a product named AL63 (produced in my own home town of Berkhamsted) was issued and with which everyone was to dust the linings of battle dresses etc. Whatever effect it had on lice, it certainly took the skin off sensitive parts of the body if applied too liberally!

23.)	There would be few members of the squadron, whatever their rank or trade, who did not share the view of Malta expressed by Greggs in his diary.

The airmen certainly felt and indeed were, very much out of things at Hal Far, at the eastern end of the island. Transport was at a premium and anyway there was 'nowhere to go'. We had billets at Birzebuggia, and where our cooks had a most difficult time eking out the apparently smaller rations supplied from the Middle East; smokers cursed the Indian 'V' cigarettes – often full of weevils. For a treat, as well as an anti-scorbutic measure, we were issued fortnightly an eight-ounce tin of peardrops, made in Palestine; there was no chocolate or beer for airmen. It was possible in the first two weeks of our stay in Malta to bathe in the sea, and we even managed to visit the wreck of the 'Ohio' of Malta convoy fame, but when our small bays began to fill up with troop carriers (51 Highland Division), swimming was abandoned on grounds of hygiene.

Up at the airfield at Hal Far, the Squadron was extremely busy fighting the air war – as part of 324 Wing which had been placed under command of 211 Group of the prestigious Desert Air Force – over both Sicily and the intervening water. Many successes were recorded, but most unfortunately the squadron lost Flight Lieutenant Prytherch over the sea; he was seen to ditch but could not be found. 'Pryth' had been in '72' as a Sergeant Pilot at Biggin Hill in 1940/1 and had been a popular Flight Commander.

At Hal Far too, on 20 June, we caught a distant glimpse of the King, as he passed by on the far side of the airfield. On the same afternoon 'Sex' Gear, on patrol with Flying Officer Sharp, shot down an Me 109 (probably on a reconnaissance of Malta) shortly before Sharp himself was shot down, and not recovered from the sea.

24.)   The advance party of HQ 324 Wing (of which by now I was a member) crossed from Malta to Sicily on the evening of 12 July (D +2) on a Landing Craft Tank. After a smooth and uneventful crossing we landed at a beach in the Pachino peninsula where the direction posts erected by the 51st Highland Division were still in position. Our Landing Craft Tank was in the same flotilla as one commanded by my brother, but he was at sea when we sailed and so I missed him; we met next in 1946.

On 12 July, 72 Squadron was in action over Sicily from Malta and destroyed three aircraft over Cassabile. We had seen nothing of the Luftwaffe on our way over to Sicily, although we passed near to a large vessel with a serious list; it looked like a small carrier but post-war research has thrown no light on its identity.

From the beaches we were soon on our way to Comiso (liberated 11 July) via Ragusa, where having been recognised as RAF, we were subjected to some very dirty looks, fist shaking, and no doubt verbal abuse in Italian, by what we judged to be some kind of political gathering.

We trod warily after our arrival at Comiso on 13 July; it was plain even to our unpractised eye that booby traps and anti-personnel bombs had been strewn around by the departing Germans. On the other hand, the still-warm loaves that we found in the cook-house ovens and the uniforms left behind in the aircrew quarters, suggested a hurried departure. We greatly admired, but did not loot, the light-weight foldable metal bed which seemed to be on general issue to Luffwaffe men, but we took over immediately as an 'intelligence trailer', an Italian mobile 'Met' trailer, timber panelled and expensively laid out; we located it about a mile away alongside the Wing's medical centre, under Squadron Leader Russell and of which Sergeant Crowe, formerly of 72, was NCO in charge.

25.)   324 Wing stayed at Comiso only until 30 July, when it took over Pachino, vacated by 244 Wing which had moved on to Lentini, as indeed had our sister Wing, 322.

An abiding memory of Pachino's airstrip – a dusty track carved out of vineyards bearing largely inedible grapes – is that of the afternoon of 1 August when five or six American Liberators made emergency landings. We did not know at the time but their aircraft had been part of a force of 192 Liberators (including some 'lent' by the 8th USAAF in the UK) which had set out at 0400 hours that morning to bomb at low level, the vital (to the Germans) oil production complex at Ploesti in Rumania, a round trip of about 2,000 miles. Incidentally, the runway at Pachino was of insufficient length to receive these heavy bombers and some overshot into Squadron dispersal areas. Across the strip one could see airmen scattering in all directions as these stricken giants bore down on them; some aircraft had seriously wounded crew aboard. Fifty four Liberators were shot down and some 532 aircrew were posted either as killed or missing. Oil production at Ploesti, which supplied a large part of German oil requirements, was never the same again.

On 17 August, the day on which fighting ended, I was flown out of Sicily to Tripoli. I had fallen sick at Comiso and I owe a debt of gratitude both to S/L Russell (SMO) and to Sgt Crowe for looking after me, before it was deemed necessary for me to be evacuated. I travelled in the rear turret of a Bristol Bombay, operated by an Australian Comm. Squadron. At Tripoli I was taken to the RAF hospital there before being moved again at the beginning of September – this time by Dakota – to No. 5 RAF Hospital Heliopolis, near Cairo. All this was some time before I was posted – in February, 1944 ostensibly for reasons of health – to a 'warm and dry' station which turned out to be Baghdad and which I reached in a Vickers Valentia! It was in Baghdad that I came across graphic evidence of 72 Squadron's tour of duty in Iraq (as well as Persia) in 1917/18, and in the course of which it was based for a time at Tikrit on the Tigris, a city which has since become notorious as the birthplace of the infamous Saddam Hussain. I had an interesting and important job to do in Baghdad as a junior member of the Combined Intelligence Centre at GHQ Paiforce, but I yearned for news of the Squadron. I was in occasional touch with Sgt Jack Walters who told me that a lot of my kit had been lost at sea, and in June 1944 I was fortunate enough to meet in Cairo, "Danny" Daniels who had then only recently relinquished command of the Squadron in Italy. It was from him that I first heard news of Greggs Farish's adventure at Nettuno.

Background Notes
on Operations 1943 – 45

OPERATION HUSKY

The decision that an Anglo-American force should invade Sicily in July 1943 was made at the Casablanca Conference of January 1943, but the military plan was not approved until almost the end of the Tunisian campaign in early May. The operation – code name HUSKY – involved the landing on twenty six beaches on the southern and south-eastern corner of Sicily of 150,000 troops in the first three days, and a subsequent build-up to about 478,000. The 1st Canadian Division (embarked in the Clyde) and 5th Division (from Paiforce) were to join General Montgomery's 8th Army (almost 250,000 strong) and which was to be landed from near Cassabile southwards to the Pachino peninsula) whereas the US 5th Army (under General George Patton and more than 220,000 strong) was to land between Licata and Scoglitti.

D-day was to be 10 July, and both Army Commanders planned the use of airborne troops to capture key points ahead of their line of advance, but unfortunately these landings mostly went wrong, due to a combination of bad weather, faulty navigation and even 'flak' from Allied shipping.

'Husky' convoys sailed from points as varied as Suez, The Clyde and the East Coast of the USA, as well as from within the Mediterranean itself, and involved some 1,325 vessels of all sizes (carrying with them about 1800 landing craft). Protection was supplied by no less than 6 British battleships, 15 cruisers, 128 destroyers (71 British) and 35 smaller escorts, as well as 2 Fleet carriers with 4 squadrons of Fleet Air Arm fighters with which to provide immediate cover over the beaches. Remarkably only six ships were lost at sea, but these included two carrying 500 vehicles of the Canadian Division.

By comparison, in early July, there were almost 32,000 German Army troops and 30,000 Luftwaffe personnel (including many AA gunners) in Sicily under Italian command; but by about 20 July, and after Hitler had sent in two more divisions, it had become clear that few of the 200,000 Italian troops present were prepared to fight. In fact, it was the anti-war coup staged in Rome, and resulting in Mussolini's downfall on 25 July, which led Hitler to decide upon a fighting withdrawal to Messina for all the German forces.

Implementation of the air plan for 'Husky' began after the fall of Tunis in mid-May with the systematic bombing of enemy airfields in Sicily and beyond as well as of strategic targets, some of which were also visited by the UK-based Bomber Command. Nearer to D-day, efforts were concentrated on attacking airfields in Sicily, and on attempting to provoke the Luftwaffe fighters into combat with the numerically superior Spitfire squadrons based in Malta, including '72' operating from Hal Far.

However, in view of the limited range of most of the 600 aircraft based in Malta, some doubt had been cast on the wisdom of General Montgomery's plan which was perceived as giving ports undue priority over airfields in southern Sicily. But the early capture of Pachino for use by 244 Wing of the Desert Air Force and of Comiso for use by 324 Wing and others, really meant that it was the turn of the Axis forces to fight 'under a canopy of hostile air power'. On D-day there were no more than 500 (including 110 Italian) aircraft available to oppose the landings, but between D-day and 17 July, the enemy had no more than 170 serviceable aircraft. Furthermore between 28 and 17 August (when hostilities ended) the Luftwaffe had lost a further 216 machines; indeed between mid-May and mid-August, some 800 German aircraft had been accounted for in the air, and almost 500 were found abandoned on airfields in Sicily.

By contrast, the Allied Air Forces in the Mediterranean could muster some 2,500 aircraft and in flying 27,000 sorties over Sicily, lost some 250 aircraft. It remains to be said, however, that despite much Allied superiority, the Luftwaffe still had an occasional sting left in its tail; for example, off the beaches, German bombers sank two US warships as well as a British hospital ship and seven merchantmen, while on 11/12 August, and in a well planned raid, enemy bombers destroyed about 30 aircraft of 239, 244, and 322 Wings on the ground at Lentini; 324 Wing itself was not at Lentini but at Pachino.

A detailed description of the land fighting lies outside the scope of this note, but in broad terms the military plan involved the 8th Army in clearing the island by advancing east and west of Mt Etna towards Messina, with the US 7th Army taking up a support rôle on the 8th Army's rear and left flank, as it pressed forward to the North coast. In fact, having cleared the south-east corner and captured Syracuse within three days, General Montgomery made a bold move against Catania, the gateway to Messina, some 60 miles away up the east coast road. But this road was blocked by the Germans, and so the 8th Army moved to the west side of Etna and called up its reserve division from North Africa, as did General Patton also, in preparation for a strike by his Army along the northern coastal route to Messina, having already taken the main ports of Trapani and Palermo in the far west of the island.

This major attack was planned for 1 August, but on 25 July came the dismissal of Mussolini and as a consequence of this development Hitler ordered his forces to make a series of fighting retreats to Messina, and to get away from there to Calabria. Between 11 and 17 August a total of 40,000 Germans and 60,000 Italians got away and took with them large quantities of weapons. Some 5,000 Germans were captured and 125,000 Italians laid down their arms and the Sicilians amongst them sought to make their way home (as we discovered when sticking rifles into the side of corn carts passing through the airfield at Comiso!). Allied battle casualties totalled 23,000, including 10,000 Americans. It remains to be said that the Axis evacuation of Sicily was allowed to proceed without any sustained Allied attempt at interdiction over the flak-ridden Straits of Messina and that the German Staff was very worried about the proposal of a landing in Calabria even while the Sicilian campaign was in progress. Such a move however, did not materialise until 3 September – 'Baytown'.

In Sicily, there were in fact as many Allied casualties from malaria and sand fly fever as arose in actual combat. Certainly, on the squadron at Pachino, the sick-rate from these two scourges was in excess of 60% despite the availability of the anti-malaria prophylactic 'Mepacrine' which all ranks were supposed to take regularly. The RAF's mobile (i.e. tented) hospital was at full stretch in the heat and dust of Pachino and found itself dealing with some cases of the more dangerous 'cerebral malaria', believed to have been contracted when some ships of the Clyde convoy, which included some RAF Regiment personnel, 'marked time' off Algiers.

OPERATIONS BAYTOWN, SLAPSTICK, GIANT (1) AND AVALANCHE

Plans had been drawn up since May, but not until 20 July 1943 did the Americans finally accede to the British view that Allied Armies should press ahead with the invasion of the Italian mainland as soon as possible after achieving victory in Sicily (17 August), having regard particularly to the fact that by the year's end, seven Allied Divisions (four American and three from the 8th Army), many landing craft (of which there was an insufficiency everywhere) as well as aircraft of the US IVth Air Force, and some RAF squadrons, were due to move to the UK in preparation for Overlord.

In finalising its plans, the Allied High Command was aware that since early August the Italians secretly had been seeking an Armistice, which was in fact signed at Cassabile on 3 September, but not announced until 8 September in the hope that in the interval it would be possible for the Italian Army to so arrange their disposition that they would be able to support an airborne operation ('Giant' 1) against Rome, thereby threatening the future of all the substantial German forces to the south of Rome including those already placed in position by Field Marshal Kesselring (Air Commander in Italy) to oppose a major landing, which he guessed, rightly, would be made in the Bay of Salerno ('Avalanche'). But the Italians sat on their hands and made no worthwhile preparations; as a result the airborne 'drops' by the US 82nd Parachute Division were called off on 8 September, only hours before aircraft were due to take off for Rome from Sicily. What was not known then was that Hitler, having anticipated Italian 'treachery' had at the end of July begun to move eight divisions into Northern Italy to reinforce Kesselring's forces in the south, and had also despatched a tough Parachute Division from France to take up position at Ostia, outside Rome. There was, no doubt, a sigh of relief also amongst the pilots of 239 and 244 Wings, who apparently had been earmarked to go to the assistance of the 82nd Airborne, once the latter had landed in the Rome area.

The landings at Salerno on 9 September ('Avalanche') were undertaken by the US 5th Army, commanded by General Mark Clark and reinforced by the 8th Army's 10th Corps, originally earmarked for a landing in the Gulf of Gioa ahead of the advance being made northwards from Reggio to Calabria since 3 September, when to launch 'Baytown', 13 Corps had landed unopposed around Reggio to clear the straits of Messina for Allied shipping, it was then to move northwards as quickly as possible to put pressure on German troops resisting at Salerno, some 300 miles away, and which 13 Corps duly reached on 16 September. As usual 13 Corps enjoyed the full support of the Desert Air Force, which was quick to move its Squadrons onto the mainland. Furthermore Desert Air Force officers accompanied the 1st British Parachute Division when it landed unopposed at Taranto on 9 September in Operation 'Slapstick'. The Paras and RAF had been transported from Bizerta in cruisers as well as in the mine-layer Abdiel, which herself struck a mine in Taranto harbour. Not only 48 crew members but also more than 100 Paras were drowned as a result, but the survivors, and the DAF Officers, pressed on to capture the ports of Bari and Brindisi and to set up airfields there, preparatory to the seizure at the end of September of the vital airfield complex at Foggia. But 324 Wing played no part in any of these operations, since they had been placed (7 September) under the operational command of the US 12th Tactical Air Command, in preparation for 'Avalanche'; accordingly '72' had moved to Falcone on the north coast of Sicily.

The announcement of the Italian armistice was made on 8 September while the 'Avalanche' convoys were at sea, and the reception of such news would not have helped to concentrate the minds of the 55,000 American and British troops involved in the landings; there was to be a follow-up of 110,000.

The formidable naval escorts included six battleships and 111 destroyers; in the hope of achieving surprise General Clark chose to forego a preliminary naval and air bombardment. But this decision was misplaced for, as indicated earlier,

Kesselring had anticipated such a landing and had deployed his Panzers to keep a watchful eye on the Bay of Salerno.

A notable feature was the presence also of five British escort carriers carrying 100 Seafires, with which to provide the convoy's protection until such time as the 400 Airfield constructors and RAF men who landed on D-day had prepared airstrips in the bridgehead for use by single-engined fighters – previously operating from Sicily with drop tanks – to enable them to patrol over the bridgehead, albeit for not more than 25 minutes per sortie.

No detailed review of the fighting will be offered here, but it was extremely fierce and costly for the first seven days and to quote the Duke of Wellington, it turned out to be "a damned close run thing"; indeed at one point General Clark apparently contemplated the evacuation of his 6th Corps. But reinforcements by sea and air (including elements of the 82nd Airborne Division) arrived to stem the tide, as did also the 15 inch guns of HMS *Warspite*. Furthermore, on 14 September, all available bombers of the Mediterranean Strategic Air Force were called in, with the Tactical bomber force, to fly a total of 1900 bomber sorties over the enemy lines in the bridgehead.

By 16 September, the enemy had begun to withdraw, not least to avoid being outflanked by the troops of 13 Corps advancing from Calabria to make contact with the Allies' bridgehead forces. Also on 16 September, the battleship HMS *Warspite* was hit and seriously damaged off Salerno, by a 3,000 lb German (HS293) radio controlled bomb, launched from a "stand off" high-flying mother aircraft. Both HE 1775 and DO 217s were used in this role, and on 17 September the ubiquitous Roy Hussey intercepted and destroyed two DO 217s in the Salerno area. His Number Two, Rodney Scrase, recalls watching their crew baling out into the sea.

Also part of the air plan for 'Avalanche', 324 Wing had moved north from Pachino on 29 August and 72 Squadron went first to Piambianco, and then on to Cassala on 2 September, before moving to Falcone.

It was of course at Cassala on 1 September that Greggs Farish received the head injuries which caused him to miss the Salerno 'show' and led to his enforced departure from 72 Squadron as "non-effective, sick".

From Falcone the Squadron flew a number of three hour sweeps to the bridgehead, and it was one of the first to land in the bridgehead (13 September) to begin extensive operations from Tusciano, a strip in close proximity to the guns of the Royal Horse Artillery, which were themselves in constant action.

The intention at Salerno was to move out of the bridgehead quickly to capture the port of Naples (20 miles away) and its airfields. 10 Corps entered Naples after hard fighting on 10 October, and by 12 October 324 Wing had moved into Capodichino airfield, and from where after three adventurous months of city life, it was moved out on 7 January 1944 to a new strip prepared at Lago, between Capua and the coast, and from where it was to operate for the next five months in support of the US 5th Army's strongly resisted but eventually successful effort to reach Rome on 4 June.

OPERATION SHINGLE

It was in fact to assist the US 5th Army, held up by strong German resistance on the Garigliano and Rapido rivers, with Cassino in between, that a seaborne landing behind the Germans and south of Rome, was decided upon in December 1943; it was to take place on the beaches around Anzio on 22 January, and bore the codename 'Shingle'. the 115,000 troops involved came mostly from the US 6th Corps, substantially reinforced by the British 1st Division (ex 1st Army), the ubiquitous Special Service Brigade, and the 46th Royal Tank Regiment. They were all transported from the Naples area in 250 landing craft.

At Anzio, and unlike both Sicily and Salerno, the air plan placed no emphasis on the early acquisition of airstrips in the bridgehead (about 17 miles long, 7 miles deep and with a perimeter of 26 miles), nor on the presence of carrier borne aircraft, largely for the reason that Anzio had been judged to be within easy range of the airstrips near the mouth of the Volturno, such as Lago. This strip was used by 324 Wing throughout 'Shingle', and operationally the Wing continued to be under the operational direction of the US 64th Fighter Wing, part of the renamed 12th Tactical Air Command (TAC).

The Allies held some 2,700 aircraft available to support the 'Shingle' operation, and about half of which had moved from North African bases to Foggia, with most of the others based in Sardinia and Corsica which the Germans had abandoned in November 1943.

On the enemy's side the Germans, on D-day, had available an estimated 200 aircraft, of which about 175 were fighters;

however only approximately 75, based around Rome, were serviceable on the day. But on Hitler's orders, over 100 bombers were drafted into Northern Italy from France and Greece, and even 'glider-bomb' carrying aircraft were placed on readiness at Bordeaux. German fighter bombers flew about 100 sorties on D-day, but the main attacks came almost nightly from 24 January to the end of the month when up to 100 bombers attacked the bridgehead; 14 bombers were shot down by the Beaufighters of 255 and 600 Squadrons (fellow squadrons at Souk el Arba). On 28 January a radio controlled 'glider bomber' launched by a Dornier 217 hit a US ship.

Over the beaches at Anzio and beyond, 324 Wing had their share of what actual combat there was, and accounted for a number of enemy fighters. One squadron of the Wing – 111 – had been re-equipped in early January with Spitfire IXs powered by the new Merlin 66 engines designed to provide more power below 20,000 feet but which unaccountably gave so much trouble in 111's hands that the squadron was 'stood down', pending the arrival of experts from Rolls Royce, Derby, to investigate the cause of these serious problems besetting 111, and which had led to a number of emergency landings at Nettuno, where there was little prospect of engine failures being rectified in the short term.

At Nettuno it so happened that there was a need for a landing strip for use by Allied Ambulance and communication aircraft, and one was laid down with pierced steel plating (PSP). It had also been used as a forward base by the 307th Fighter Squadron of the 64th Fighter Wing for a few days, but by 10 February it had become untenable for the 307th on account of its greatly increased vulnerability to

German artillery fire. Thus it had reverted to being an emergency landing strip available for use by 324 Wing, amongst others, by Lago-based pilots in difficulty over the bridgehead.

At Salerno, there was no naval or air bombardment to herald the landings at Anzio, which took the Germans completely by surprise; in fact the Germans had been expecting a landing north of Rome. In any event, Hitler's immediate response was to activate contingency plans for the instant reinforcement of Italy, while Kesselring's own brilliant staff work – notwithstanding the attentions of the Allied Air Forces – contrived to ensure the prompt arrival of sufficient forces at the bridgehead to contain the first Allied attempts to advance on the Alban Hills and to threaten Rome. No attempt will be made to describe the course of the battle, which lasted in fact until early March, and was like Salerno, 'a damned close run thing'; an additional division, the British 5th Division commanded by Major General Gerald Templer (later known as 'The Tiger of Malaya'), was transferred to the bridgehead from the Garigliano river line. On 14 February there was a lull in the fighting, as the Germans were preparing a new attack on 16 February; meanwhile on 14 February, elements of 56 Division were continuing to arrive by sea. It was on the same day that Flight Lieutenant 'Greggs' Farish who had been Engineer Officer of 111 Squadron since November 1943 following his return to duty after a serious head injury (incurred at Cassala on 1 September while serving with 72 Squadron) felt impelled on account of 111's engine problems to make his own way to the shell-pocked and almost deserted strip at Nettuno by flying solo for the first time ever in 111's 'spare' Spitfire VC.

Flight Lieutenant Farish was flown out of Nettuno a day or so later in a US Fairchild courier aircraft, in the circumstances described in his diary and there is no need to say more here that while Nettuno had seen the end of Greggs Farish's most fruitful association with 111 and 72 Squadrons, as well as with 324 Wing as a whole, the Wing had not seen the last of Nettuno, for a little later on the strip was used as an 'overnight' base.

Eventually after much hard fighting and continuous air attack, an entry into Rome was achieved by the US 5th Army on 4 June 1944. Thereafter, on account of its continuous attachment to the 12th Tactical Air Command, 324 Wing found its future bound up with the preparations being made for an Allied landing in the south of France (Dragoon) in August.

By this time Greggs Farish had been found work as the EO of a Communication Flight at Caserta and what follows now is certainly not an attempt to 'write in' a final chapter of Greggs' diary, but a brief chronicle of what happened to 324 Wing and its squadrons from the time of Greggs' departure from the scene in February to the triumphant arrival of the Wing in Austria in May 1945. This chronicle should be read as belated recognition of all those 'on the squadrons', who unlike Greggs and the writer of these notes, were able to see it through all the way from Algiers to Austria, in what must sometimes have seemed to be a remarkably long and uncomfortable two and a half years.

OPERATION DRAGOON

'Dragoon', the invasion of Southern France by an Allied
Force, predominately an American and Free French expedition but supported by a British Parachute Brigade (which
dropped at Le Moy), numerous Royal Naval escorts, notably
five escort carriers, as well as 324 Wing, began on 15 August.

By 20 August, 324 Wing including 72 Squadron, was
operating from a dusty airstrip carved out of a vineyard at
Ramatuelle, between Frejus and Ste. Maxime, (having
previously been at Calvi in Corsica since 20 July following
short spells north of Rome at Tarquina (14 June), Grosseto (25
June) and Piambini (5 July). On 25 August, 324 were ordered
to a landing ground near Sisteron, high up on the Route
Napoleon between Cannes and Grenoble. There was a
shortage of targets in the air, but on the ground between 25
August and 10 September, the Wing 'bagged' 150 enemy
transports and even one 'Tiger' tank. On 7 September the
Wing moved to Lyons/Bron but found few targets and a plan
to move on to Besanscon did not mature.

On 12 September, control of the 12th Tactical Air
Command passed to the US Ninth Air Force operating in
France under the command of General Eisenhower,
Supreme Allied Commander of 'Overlord'. But hopes that
324 Wing might continue to fly with the 64th Fighter Wing
(from bases even closer to home!) were dashed when orders
were received to return immediately to Peretola, Florence (via
La Jasse and Corsica), where their aircraft would be modified
to carry bombs. After a somewhat desultory month at
Florence, the Wing moved east to Rimini on 13 November,

to return to the bosom of the Desert Air Force, operating in support of the 8th Army.

From Rimini, '72' moved to Ravenna on 17 February 1945, and to much practice in the use of new techniques of close support for the Army, of which 324's former 'Wingco Flying', (by then Group Captain HSL Dundas) had become a leading exponent as CO of 244 Wing. Such techniques were put to outstandingly good effect in the final Allied offensive of the Italian campaign – 'Grapeshot' – which began on 9 April and ended on 2 May, by which time not only the German forces in the Po valley had been destroyed, but the German Commander (Vietinghoff) had surrendered all the German Forces in Italy and Southern Austria. Such a crushing victory was achieved not without loss; the Allies incurred 16,000 including 3,000 British battle casualties, and the Germans about 20,000 including many as a result of action from the air.

On the air side, the Allied Air Forces flew a total of 865,000 sorties in the Italian campaign and in the last seven months dropped half a million tons of bombs. The Allies lost some 8,000 aircraft during the two and a half year's campaign; the actual number of Allied airmen lost is not known but bearing in mind the numbers of heavy bombers used may well have been not less than 12,000.

So ended the war for 324 Wing, and its squadrons, which had been at Rivolta since 4 May and by the time VE day was declared in Northern Europe on 8 May, 324 Wing was preparing to move to Klagenfurt as it did on 11 May. In May also, the Wing went down to Udine to take part in the Desert Air Force's farewell fly past, and there followed a number of moves around Austria and to the Trieste area before, at Tissano on 30 December 1946, the Squadron was disbanded, only to be reformed as a Vampire (F1) Squadron at Odiham on 1 February 1947; in fact 130 Squadron was renumbered '72'.

Thus ends this chronicle of the 'caravan' route taken by 324 Wing and the two 'mobile' squadrons 72 and 111, of which Greggs Farish had been such an important member up to the time of his departure from the Wing in February 1944.

The writer of this note would like to leave the last word, to Winston Churchill, who on 30 April 1945 sent a telegram to Field Marshal Alexander, the Allied Supreme Commander in Italy, extracts of which are given below:

> "I rejoice in the magnificently planned and executed operation of the 15th Army Group ... resulting in the complete destruction or capture of all enemy forces south of the Alps.

> "Never I suppose have so many nations advanced and manoeuvred in one line victoriously – British, American, New Zealanders, South Africans, British Indians, Poles, Jews, Brazilians and a strong force of liberated Italians have all marched together ...

> "This grand finale battle in Italy will long stand out in history as one of the most famous episodes of the Second World War.

> "Pray give my heartfelt congratulations to all your commanders and principal officers of all services, and above all, to the valiant and ardent troops whom they have led with such skill."

20 March 1944:
A Court Martial and its Sequel

The text that follows was revised by the author in 1995.

There is a certain stigma attached to the words "Court Martial" by reason of the public's assumption of guilt before the trial. As a result of my necessarily pleading guilty to the Charge under Section 39A, an act likely to cause damage to an aircraft belonging to his Majesty and of which I had no doubt whatsoever, there would be no argument in court on this point. I was guilty of that one and all I could do would be to throw myself onto the Court's clemency, if any. But when it came to the second, and to me more serious charge under Section 40, i.e. conduct prejudicial to good order and discipline, it seemed to me that there were circumstances which should be brought out in court; after all I had by my own actions not only given JU-U back to 111 Squadron in serviceable condition but I had rendered JU-A serviceable under most adverse conditions and had it flown back to Lago safely, and surely a good pilot and a Spitfire IX are worth quite a lot. Also I had fixed up two more Spitfires which had landed at Nettuno before the RAF was aware that the aerodrome had been abandoned by the US 307th Fighter Wing. It happened that these forced landings were easy to fix, but it was handy to be there right on the spot with my specialised knowledge and get the aircraft and pilots away quickly before a shell hit either one of them.

The Intelligence Officer of 111 Squadron at that time happened to be F/O HGF Buckton, who was not only an excellent Intelligence Officer but also quite an experienced member of the Bar in civilian life so having talked my case over with him thoroughly, he agreed to become my "friend of the accused" in court for Charge 40. The particular part of the charge that we wanted to deny was the wording "conduct to the prejudice of good order and discipline".

After all, saving four pilots and three aircraft while under shell fire scarcely seemed to us to be contrary to good order and discipline, regardless of formal regulations, and so, Buckton and I started preparing our case to bring out the whole story of my actions.

The Prosecutor for the Advocate General's Office was S/Lr TU Liddle and the Board itself consisted of G/Capt CP Green, President; W/C J Wallace; W/C RR Thompson, among whom there were one DSO and three DFCs, S/L AH Porter and F/Lt J Macfarlane.

Thus F/O Buckton and I were up against quite some opposition had the court wished to take a dim view of our defence. But when we got to the nitty gritty of the facts we found to my pleasure and almost surprise, that, judging by the voluminous questions from the Court itself, the pilots who really constituted the Board were far more interested in how I had managed to fly a first solo in a Spitfire landing it safely, than they were in hanging me.

I had offended every rule in the Pilot's Union it seemed to me, and yet these pilots were all empathetic. With Buckton's shrewd help on cross-examination, we were able to bring out all the ameliorating circumstances, including Tom Hughes' early training of my flying the Pisser, without which the whole thing would have been impossible. Fortunately both for him and me, Tom had never let me go solo in the Pisser. During most of the cross-examinations Buckton ran rings around the Prosecutor who seemed to take a more legalistic approach when he could, but the Board was just not interested in his concerns but only with the details of how I had done it at all. Realising I was essentially talking with pilots, I held nothing back in my answers, from the dangerous take-off, flaps in the wrong position, to the landing *à la* Tom's training in the Pisser.

The Prosecutor nearly surprised me on only one occasion: this was more than half way through when he suddenly accused me of having performed the whole thing out of "an overweening conceit in my own ability".

To the inference of this question I answered with one word, "No", and by that time I had sufficiently described the risks I had taken including those on the ground after my landing to make it, in the prevailing atmosphere of the Court, impossible for the Prosecutor to follow up his nasty question. I am glad I kept that answer to one word. To enlarge on the question might have been fatal for there was indeed an element of vanity, or at least pig-headedness, included in my decision to borrow JU-U and take off.

During the War, apart from Squadron pilots, I had lost two personal friends whom I had loved dearly before the War started at all. Was I by any chance trying to compensate in some odd way for their deaths? Who knows; the motives for all decisive actions in one's life are, in my experience, rarely single but generally somewhat mixed. But this was neither the time nor the place to go into complicated analysis so when Buckton wisely signalled me to leave my answer with the one word "No", I just left it at that and S/L Liddle, who was in a minority of one as to whether the question was quite fair, considering there was absolutely no prior evidence already presented at this trial to back him up, did not pursue this line of questioning.

A somewhat amusing incident took place during F/O Buckton's preparation for the trial. He decided that it might be a good thing for us to have access to my medical records in case of surprise questions from the Prosecutor. He approached the Medical Officer and was told rather abruptly that such records could only be released to me and no one else, so he wrote about three-quarters of a page of explanation in his own handwriting, which was none too good, and had me sign it at the end.

The MO took one glance at Buckton's scrawl and replied without even seeing my signature on the bottom, "No, certainly not. Anyone can see from the handwriting on the application that the man if mentally deficient." At which Buckton drew himself up to his full legal height and with great dignity replied: "Thanks very much for your opinion, but the handwriting on that document happens to be my own!" The MOs at Courts Martial are unnecessarily rude; probably bored with their job together with the unfortunate assumption of automatic guilt which I mentioned as a characteristic of certain people in Courts. But after Buckton had pointed out his mistake, the MO was forced to part with his precious records.

Buckton had been a little concerned about my bang on the head from the Pisser's propeller about a year before and was just being thorough. In fact there was nothing in the records which could suggest permanent damage and neither the Prosecutor nor the Doctor brought the matter up at the trial.

After both the Prosecution and the Defence had stated that they had no more questions and the Prosecutor had declined to make a closing address, Buckton made a good address on my behalf stressing the extraordinary circumstances I had found myself in and that I had tried to get two multi-seat aircraft to take me to Anzio without success. Although there was no question but that I had broken King's Regulations by flying myself there, there are occasions when the breaking of KRs was actually in favour of good order and discipline and that this was one of those rare occasions, since the morale of some of the pilots was liable to become affected if we did not fix the problem quickly.

The only thing I wish he had brought out more strongly was the miserable report of W/O Charters on the conditions he had found at Nettuno during his visit in the morning but probably Buckton judged that these conditions (shell-fire etc. and the evacuation of the strip by the USAAF the previous day) had been sufficiently brought out during the actual trial. Certainly Charters' report weighed a lot with me. After that it was the turn of the Judge Advocate to sum up. He did so in quite a fair fashion I thought, leaving a door open for the Court to find me not guilty or guilty depending on their understanding of my difficulties and concern for Squadron morale.

After this Buckton and I were asked to leave the Court-room while the Court itself discussed their verdict or verdicts. We felt we had made a pretty good case against the second charge under Section 40 while there was just no hope under the first, Section 39 (1) (b).

In the result the RAF outwitted us. They found me guilty on both charges, but they made the punishment the same for both, namely a Severe Reprimand, and six months loss of seniority. We had pleaded guilty to the first charge anyway, but the only one we really cared about was the second charge, where I felt a moral question was involved. But now we could not distinguish between the two charges. Buckton and I went away somewhat disappointed, to put it mildly.

But there was help, which we did not know about, on the way. The findings were promulgated on March 20th 1944, but on July 31st 1944 the following notice was circulated in Daily Routine Orders: "After careful consideration the (Air) Council have formed the opinion that the sentence was too severe and they have decided in exercise of their power under Section 57 (2) of the Air Force Act, to remit that part of the sentence relating to loss of seniority."

This came only four months and eleven days after the original sentence and of course was a considerable relief for me since I would now be eligible for a Flight Lieutenant post if one ever came up. Buckton and I allowed ourselves a smile of satisfaction. At this time I was serving with 113 Mainten-ance Unit at Castellamare, the place where the Sorrento Peninsular rejoins the mainland after its tour of Sorrento itself,

Positano and Amalfi, three of the mot beautiful spots in the world. Off-shore lay Capri and Ischia and to the East, not far away, the remains of Pompeii.

I was, in my leisure moments, able to see all these places, and read about them, in the most ideal conditions, that is before the tourists got there. Today they tell me the whole area has been ruined, not only by the hoards of tourists who come there by the bus load, but also by industrial contamination, so bad coming out of Naples, that one cannot even see Vesuvius from the city. I did not, as it happens have to wait long before a Flight Lieutenant post opened up as if by magic. At Caserta (near Capua the Headquarters of Hannibal during the ancient Punic Wars) the remains of the European war was still being fought out. Eisenhower and Montgomery had been moved North to command the forthcoming invasion of Normandy, leaving behind in charge of Italian operations, Field Marshal Alexander. Both the Americans and the British ran from Caserta, Communications Squadrons to carry their "big bugs" about on special missions, particularly to Algiers and Cairo.

The British component of this group of aircraft was called Med/ME Communications Squadron and consisted of at least seven different types of aircraft, one Dakota, one ancient but very reliable Wellington with the same geodetic fuselage construction which Vickers use throughout the war and were to continue in their first civilian transport models for British European Airways, maybe a dozen Hudsons, derived by Lockheed from the Ventura bomber, maybe half a dozen Fairchild three-seaters for dispatch carrying, one Lockheed Electra, a smaller version of the Hudson but still with the characteristic triple fins at the tail and two or three Mosquitoes with their counter-rotating propellers – great speed for those times.

The CO of Med/ME Communications Squadron was in something of a jam. Although he had enough experienced pilots for the Dakota and the Wellington, there were not enough experienced ones for the other five types. Moreover he received requests for use of the Mosquitoes for sheer fun flying from senior officers at Caserta which, of course, he found it difficult to refuse. At least two Mosquitoes were crashed by pilots who had no prior experience of flying them and the Hudsons. It was always a problem to find experienced pilots who were ready for the Hudson's tendency to ground loop and so on. In addition to this there had been a number of accidents attributable to poor or non-existent maintenance on the ground, for the ground crews could not be expected to know as thoroughly as they ought to, so many different types. Into this mess the Squadron Adjutant happened one lunch time to remark to the CO.

"You know, we have been pretty dumb when you think about it. Right here in MAAF, we have one of the most experienced Squadron Maintenance Engineers in the RAF. I mean Farish who is presently spinning his wheels down at Castellamare on motor vehicles. Why don't we get him posted to Med/ME. He has four years direct experience on aircraft maintenance."

"You mean the one that flew the Spitfire," says the CO, "do you think the powers that be will ever let him near an aeroplane again?"

"I don't see why not", replied the Adjutant. "Let me have a go."

"OK, see what you can do", replied the CO.

Within a week the Adjutant had seen the Personnel people at MAAF who thought this a good idea and so, on October 15th, 1944 I found myself posted, as a substantive Flight Lieutenant to Med/ME Communications Squadron in the position of Engineer Officer, and with instructions straight from the top, to straighten out the maintenance of the Squadron. I might add that it certainly needed stricter maintenance and I gave it all I had got, with greatly improved results as regards aircraft reliability. Moreover, I received the right to a 15cwt van which came with the job. My luck was certainly breaking for within seven months of having been demoted I now found myself promoted to Flight Lieutenant. "Well, well", I told Buckton at the Officers' Club, "one never knows with the RAF does one?"

Buckton of course was equally delighted. But there was yet more good news to come although not immediately!

I was released from the Service with the rank of Flight Lieutenant on a Class B (early) release on 4th April 1946 in order to go back to my old Engineering College, the City and Guilds of Imperial College, London University, to finish my degree, where after a lot of grinding away at higher mathematics which I had not seen for five years, I managed to obtain my degree.

Many Years Later...

It was not until 1994 when I was in the UK to attend the first reunion of the 72 Squadron Association, that I was introduced to Reg Wyness, the very efficient Secretary of 111's Old Boys' Club. Wyness had heard of my first solo flight in a Spitfire from various sources, mostly quite unreliable, and he and Tom Hughes had been looking for me for more than seven years in order to get the true story. I had emigrated to Canada in 1952 and lost touch with my old RAF friends. One day Tom was on a cruise ship in the middle of the Indian Ocean, and ran into a fellow Engineer and asked, as was his habit by now, if the Engineer had ever heard of me. "What schools have you already tried?" the Engineer asked.

"Well, first I went through Oxford and Cambridge, I was at Cambridge myself, and then every red brick University in their reference libraries. I got a line on him from the RAF Association but their address was years out of date; I guess he had let his subscription drop."

"I happened to go to the City and Guilds College of Imperial College of London University myself", said the Engineer and added rather stiffly, "it's the best in England, the equivalent of MIT in the US. But it is small and highly specialised so you Varsity people may have never heard of it, especially as it so well disguised under both Imperial College and London University auspices. But I happen to have a list of its graduates down in my cabin. Hold on while I go and check."

The one institution with which I had kept my address up to date, largely through the encouragement of Theo Marx, their Secretary, who was still a personal friend of mine ever since our first year days after which he was rounded up by the British Security authorities as being of recent German Jewish extraction, and sent to spend the rest of the war on the Isle of Man. At his hearing, I had gone along to stand up for Theo, pointing out what a promising British student he was by now; to no avail except to make me such a good friend that we have exchanged Christmas cards ever since. Thus it was not difficult for Theo to include me, with current address in Canada in his own Directory. The Engineer came back from his cabin, grinning from ear to ear and showed Tom the entry in about the only record book he had not happened to find. "Well", said Tom, "the dates look about right so I'll write to him right away to make sure this is really Greggs." Which he promptly did and I was overjoyed to hear from him so a correspondence between Tom, Reg Wyness and myself transpired.

Most of my time on squadrons had been with '72', of which of course, Tom had been a leading member until his frightful crash. As you know by now, Tom was my bravest hero among all the pilots I had worked for, so, as a casual favour, I dug out the four dusty old notebooks which were the basis of this diary, complete with a number of photographs, stuck into them, and still myself not attributing much value to them, sent them by post to Tom. Tom was thrilled by the diaries, covered me with praise for not only their historical value but also their literary qualities, and demanded that they should be published forthwith.

Unfortunately, Tom, after his retirement, was not able to take on the editing job himself due to health reasons. Reg wanted to take it on but I had only bee with 111 about five months, at the end of which the solo flight had occurred. Both Tom and I preferred someone with a '72' background considering my much longer service with them. Tom knew Mike McCaul and suggested that he take charge. At the same time, I gave Reg permission to quote from those parts of the diaries which actually dealt with the 111 Flight and he had a good writer, Alan Crouchman, who was well known to "Flypast" as a contributor, and made an excellent précis, with my help of the actual flight. At the same time, we asked Crouchman to mention the existence of this bigger book, containing all the diaries.

This little summary of how this book got written has served to introduce all the main people who have in various parts helped me to turn the manuscript and actually, unfinished diaries, into this book; my main helper having been Mike McCaul himself. However, Reg with his good advice and thorough knowledge of King's (and later, Queen's) Regulations, became a vital adviser. In this case Reg and I were just yarning when he asked casually, "Have you ever seen your own Record of Service?"

"No", I answered, "I didn't know I could".

"By Kings Regulations, you can, and only you. You have to apply to the RAF Personnel Centre, giving your name and Service Number and they will send you a copy of it. It might be worthwhile in your case in regard to the second charge of your Court Martial. I assume you still care about it and I have known them to correct findings in the past. Send me a copy when you get it. I may be able to help with some of the interpretations and I know you will find it handy when it comes to dates of postings, etc."

So I did as Reg had suggested and was pleased to get a prompt reply from the RAF Personnel Management Centre Headquarters in Gloucester dated April 20, 1994. This document ran to four pages of quarto with entries in women's handwriting all over it. Everywhere I checked it appeared to be authentic right down to my date and place of birth, my mother's name and address as next of kin, and the correct date of my original joining up on April 4, 1941 with the august rank of Acting Pilot Officer. And my Service Number, which one never forgets was written in clear handwriting: 63124, on the top right of the second sheet. Under "Special Notes" on the fourth sheet, appeared the words in clear handwriting, uncorrected:

"A677664/44 Tried by General Court Martial, Rear Headquarters, Desert Air Force on 15-3-44 on two charges under Section 39A (1) (b) and Section (40) Air Force Act that when on active service in the field in not being a qualified pilot improperly and without authority took off and flew aircraft, likely to cause damage to aircraft, contrary to regulations. Guilty of first charge under Section 39A (1) (b) but Not Guilty of second charge under Section 40".

Well, you could have knocked me down with a feather. I compared this statement to that contained in the Official record of the Court Martial itself which had said that I had been found guilty on both charges. The Section 40 charge was the one that Buckton and I had decided to fight, on moral grounds really rather than practical ones. As I remember it the standard phrase used by the RAF contained the words, "conduct prejudicial to good order and discipline". The whole wording was such that the RAF could make the charge mean anything they wanted it to mean and it was almost impossible to beat it. I have never heard of anyone else having succeeded in doing so. Firstly I had to check with Reg from his knowledge of Queen's Regulations, which version, in case of conflict between documents, ruled – the Official transcript of a Court Martial or the Records Department's version. Reg had no difficulty in clarifying this point. "The Record as kept by the Personnel Management Centre always takes precedence," he said. "That's the final judgement."

"So that means I was actually found Not Guilty of the conduct prejudicial to good order and discipline clause," I said, "the one Buckton and I did so much to argue with the Court about." I don't know quite why, but I was jumping for joy. I only wished Buckton could be present at our celebration but Reg said that he was dead by now.

The punishment on both charges had, at the Court Martial, been rolled into one so this made no practical difference to the long-term effect of my record, which, by now, was limited to a Severe Reprimand, but morally there is a world of difference between accepting the justice of punishment to which one had pleaded guilty in the first place as compared to what had never seemed to me to be fair treatment on the second charge. So that was what G/Capt Duncan Smith must have meant when in his book *Thanks for the Memory* he said "Spanner was court martialled but got away with it". The moral effect of having become one of the few people who had ever beaten the Air Force at their own all embracing charge of "conduct prejudicial to good order and discipline" was, for me and is even at this late date, most stimulating to my self respect. I had loved my time in the RAF anyway but now my consciousness of an injustice on their part was gone, for good, and I held my head high as I left Reg's office.

Hooray for Buckton and me!

Photographs

The "MV Staffordshire" (10,618 tons), built on the Clyde in 1929, was part of convoy KMF3 which left Gourock on 14 November 1942 and reached Algiers unscathed, on 22 November. 72's ground personnel travelled on the MV Staffordshire, apparently one of about fifteen troop carriers. The convoy was heavily escorted, especially in the approaches to Gibraltar, where U-Boats had been deployed following the German failure to inflict significant damage on either KMF1 or KMF2 in waters to the north. The Staffordshire survived both heavy bombing off the Hebrides in April 1941 and the rest of the war, but was broken up in 1959. (By permission of Bibby Group, Liverpool.)

(above) The covoy lying off Algiers harbour.

(below) Creeping into Algiers harbour in order to disembark. The Navy was having a hell of a time getting ships most urgently needed in the correct order. The landing on D+13 was uneventful and I landed in my best blue, but carrying a rifle. On shore we were sorted out into our respective squadrons.

Some of 72's pilots at Maison Blanche having flown their Spitfire Vs from Algiers. Note the "pranged" Hurricane and an unmarked "Spit" on the right. Note also the four-gallon tins of petrol for refuelling. These cans pre-dated "Jerrycans" and were dangerous in that after emptying, they might be used for carrying liquids other than petrol, especially water. In fact a tin of water was inadvertently used to refuel Sex Gear's Spit, causing a sudden loss of power half way down the runway. Sex was able to make a safe crash landing. The identifiable pilots seated are: Hussey (centre left), Corbin (next to Hussey), Charnock (fourth from left), Danny Daniels and David Cox.

Souk el Arba at last, the date was 1 December 1942. The pilots had flown in from Algiers and Bone on 18 November together with some RAF Servicing Commandos, to service their aircraft pending the arrival of 72's ground staff. In fact, the original air plan had envisaged pilots and ground crews rendezvousing in Algiers on 22 November. The pilots in the photograph are (left) F/L Derek Forde, F/O Danny Daniels, and the CO S/Ldr Bobby Oxspring DFC and Bar. Living conditions were primitive; all the pilots slept together in Bell tents borrowed from the French Foreign Legion. The pilots were as glad to see us, as we were them; we were then but a group of eight MT drivers and myself.

The twin-finned transport plane between the cranes is a French Potez which had crash-landed right at the intersection of the runways at Souk el Arba before we got there and it was very much in the way of our aircraft during take off and landing. By this time more heavy equipment had arrived and I was able to borrow two cranes from the other squadron Engineering Officers so I decided to have a go at removing the obstruction. We hoisted with one crane at the tail and one on each wing. As you can imagine this was a delicate exercise of balancing so as not to overload any one of the cranes and took much gesticulating from me to the three drivers. But we managed it and carried the Potez about 100 yards out of the way.

F/L Prytherch on left, F/L Derek Forde in centre, and the CO on right, photographed at Souk el Arba. All are wearing khaki battledress, and two are carrying revolvers. Prytherch, son of a serving Admiral, had served with 72 in 1940 as a sergeant. He went on in 1943 to be a very popular Flight Commander before being lost at sea after a sweep to Sicily from Malta. Derek Forde later took over 152 Squadron. Bobby Oxpring led the Squadron both in the air and on the ground, superbly until his tour expired in April 1943.

Remarkably P/O "Robbie" Robertson was able to "walk away" but he lost an eye and was invalided home. He had previously served 72 as a very popular NCO pilot and news of his DFC at around Christmas time, pleased everyone. Robbie, however, was not pleased with his "No.2" and has not changed his mind since. Roy Hussey is the pilot without a helmet.

In the early days at Souk el Arba, and at 4 pm almost daily, but also at other random times, the Germans came over to attack our aircraft on the ground. They would particularly try to catch us whilst refuelling and rearming after a sweep; they were aware of the one and a half hour endurance of a Spit and would time their raids from the time of our take off for each sweep.

Lou, or F/L Lewis, an American who could have transferred to the USAAF but preferred to stay with 72 Squadron. The high-neck jersey he wore was a sort of trade mark. Behind him can be seen one of our RAF standard tents, 14 ft square if I remember rightly. Note the fly-sheet over this tent which was absolutely invaluable during both summer and winter. I lived in tents like this for about three years, most comfortably. It was not long before we learnt to dig them in about three feet deep and twelve feet square so as to leave a ledge for putting things on outside. They were supported by three vertical poles. "Judy" Garland, the Wing Engineer Officer at the time, who had been at the City and Guilds College with me and had taken the same structures course, got rid of the centre pole on his by stringing a cable between the two poles and supporting the centre on a mere two feet of pole. There were generally two officers to a tent; I do not remember how many airmen shared, perhaps eight, but we were never short of these marvellous homes.

And then, before Christmas it began to rain and rain. The Spit on the left is taxiing through the mud and liable to go up onto its nose at any moment. The kit lying about has not yet been put under cover.

Our oxygen apparatus; a rainy Christmas Day view. The rectangular block in the rear ground is one of our beloved Thorneycroft lorries, the only thing in these conditions, with their 4-wheel drives, which could still move.

One of our aircraft in the early stages at Souk el Arba before Squadron markings (RN) were permitted; later the RN marking would become as familiar to the enemy fighters in Tunisia as it had been over northern France as recently as August 1942.

The same aircraft as in photo 13, after a direct hit by an Me109 fighter bomber. It was beyond the scope of even our remarkably able Repair and Salvage unit.

Greggs demonstrates his solution to the hair cutting and control of lice problems.

Greggs admires the view from the top of the hill at Ghardimeou Camp, Tunisia.

The fire tender which had come in our original convoy from Bone.

The whole of A Flight's fitters draped round a Spit V at Khemis. Note that most of them, since they had to refuel the aircraft between shows, during bombing runs by Jerry, wore tin hats like the Armourers.

And here are the Armourers of A Flight to compare with the fitters. WO Norton in charge, is the man tipping his hat. These armourers had a remarkable record for lack of jammed machine guns in the air on both A and B Flights. The fact that they are all wearing tin hats whilst re-arming aircraft was because this was the time when Me109s would try to catch us defenceless and these men came in for more bombing than most sections. Note the Spit cannon-cleaning rod leaning on the left shoulder of the armourer seated with a cigarette and cup of tea. Re-arming was the longest job on squadron turn-around.

Roy Hussey and Owen Hardy on R&R (Rest and Recreation) at the old Ghademou base getting in some shooting practice, considered good training for pilots. Hardy was an outstanding shot.

Owen Hardy and Jimmy Corbin on R&R at Ghademou. They were on leave from Souk el Arba.

The stalwarts of B Flight: Cpl Spencer standing on the left, Sgt York standing on the right, who was the senior Fitter 2E and therefore my best engines man in spite of his split-pin lapse (Caption 52). In the centre of the group, neither on the ground nor standing and unfortunately a bit shaded, is the most important Halton brat on the squadron, F/Sgt Landon, who was not only my best adviser by far but also for some reason my best friend among the ground crew. I do not know what this young sprog Volunteer Reservist Engineer Officer would have been able to accomplish without Flight Sergeant Landon whose advice was generally quiet but firm and I'm glad I had enough sense to take it. His position of natural authority was analogous to that of Naldress BEM, on 111 Squadron who was equally helpful to me later.

This was our first scoreboard. A Me 109 fuselage which had been shot down by our overhead patrol. Note the words painted between the cross bar of the German identification black cross, "22 Dest", meaning 22 destroyed by that time, namely mid December.

The MT Drivers and the Armourers competed for the position of the toughest section of the squadron. Cpl Jenkins is standing fourth from left, with Bill L ... , the one who had to be invalided home (8) after the Beaufighter bombing, standing behind him. Ginger, always the cheeriest and most willing, is on the left. Grigg, really a Fitter 2, is in the centre and F/Sgt Carver, wearing a tin hat and, of course, the boss, is on the right. Note the nose of our precious Thorneycroft on the left.

Here is a better photograph of F/Sgt Landon sitting on the wing of "B", a Spitfire V, together with his Sergeant Fitter, the energetic Sgt Lancaster, Cpl Spencer and Cpl "Chick" Fowler (injured at Kasserine), the backbone of B Flight. F/Sgt Landon, awarded a well-merited BEM, was much more than just a servicing Flight Commander.

Flight Sergeant Mann of A Flight. He came out as a Sergeant rigger, never having seen a Spitfire before. Being one of those wonderful brats trained at Halton, it did not take him long to learn. He once worked all night up in the hills by lorry headlights to get a stern frame off a crash which we needed for another aircraft. Next day, having got the other Spitfire serviceable again at Souk el Arba, a piece of bomb shrapnel ruined the whole job.

Mann taught the whole squadron how to pitch bivouac tents in the rain on the beach at Algiers. He and Landon were the two best campaigners I ever knew, one in charge of each flight. They were both awarded the British Empire Medal as also was Naldress of 111 Squadron. This photograph shows clearly the large white Vokes air cleaners with which these aircraft were fitted for service in sandy conditions. The Spit IXs which came later carried no air cleaners. The Me109s had the best, a device which could be by-passed once in the air, since the Vokes for all its bulk did detract from engine performance. My own adventures with cleaners for the IXs are described in the diary.

Sgt Sollit and the Egg Man.

The approaches to the farmhouse at Souk el Khemis where, in January 1943, we moved onto new airstrips which the Sappers and Pioneers had prepared. They were still flooded in February, but eventually dried out. Note the row of tents on the higher ground to the right, and the "Thorney" ploughing on regardless. The "Thorney" is about level with the Orderly Room out of sight on the right. The Colon and his wife were good enough to clear a room at the back of the house for us to use as the Squadron Warrant Officers' office. The new strips were built of Sommerfeld tracking ("chicken wire" netting) on sandy soil, which made such a difference after the mud of Souk el Arba. Sommerfeld tracking was superseded by the American pierced steel planking (PSP), which was used extensively in Italy, both on American and RAF "strips".

A view of the country around our "rest camp" at Ghademou. The airman on the left remains unidentified but his companion is none other than the photographer A ... .

This is a composite group standing on the steps of the Orderly Room, itself a part of M Columbat's farmhouse. Those wearing steel helmets were from the Flights (ie Gregg's men) who had been called up for some reason. Some Orderly Room staff and the two Squadron photographers are in the picture on the extreme left behind W/O Elton, and Cpls Pollard and Husthwaite. One of the photographers (in glasses) was named Bartholomew, but his co-photographer is recalled only as A ... , a Channel Islander.

A disused railway line ran behind the farm at Khemis and this was its railway station. We used it as our Officers' Mess. A few destitute Italian settlers lived nearby and gladly did our laundry to earn a much needed crust. The amount of soap we were required to supply suggested that it may also have been used to supplement their diet!

The Orderly Room Staff. Tiny, the Adjutant in charge, is the big man second from right, back row. L to R, Cpl Fletcher, Cpl Husthwaite, Cpl Yonge, Cpl Pollard, LAC McCaul, AC Roberts, AC Hedger, F/Lt Le Petit, Sgt Shemming, and Sgt Walters. Tiny was a very capable administrator and leader, an executive with a tobacco company before the war. By 1944 he had risen through merit to become Wing Commander for the whole of 324 Wing. When we got our Spit IXs we found no technical manuals for them but the other Spit IX squadron on No 81 Wing had a set. With our Orderly Room going full tilt, we were able to copy all three (half-inch thick) manuals in two days and return the originals on the third day; an example of the good squadron spirit on 72.

The residence of F/O Paddy Griffith, the Medical Officer. His tent was well dug in, he had his own latrine screen, and, in this photograph, he was using his canvas camp bath. His visitor is believed to have been F/L Le Cheminant.

The Sergeant Pilots of the Squadron in March 1943. W/O Sexton Gear is standing second from right. On the right-hand end of those standing are Scotty and Frampton. Crouching, also on the right, are Roy Hussey and Griffiths. They were a wonderful lot.

Flight Sergeant Daw (second from left), NCO ic. Servicing Echelon of 72 Squadron, and five of his men, attend the site of an overturned Spitfire. Echelon did great work and were responsible for manufacturing the filters described in the diaries; see also photograph 48.

February 1943; the Squadron pig had just been killed, not without difficulty, by Cpl "Polly" Pollard on the extreme left. Cpl Husthwaite stands next to him, with AC ?Whitfield in the helmet. The others are farm employees, surprisingly eager to help. The airmen all had at least one delicious meal as a result.

F/S Horner on right and his assistant (Corporal ?Grayson) outside the main stores marquée at Souk el Khemis. They normally had to be stocked from Souk el Arba which meant one of our Thorneys had to use Messerschmidt Alley to get there and back. It was rare though if they did not have in stock, what was needed on the flight line. Major repairs by Echelon might give them a little more trouble.

The original pilot's headquarters. Note the board beside the tent pole, used for plotting the position of each pilot for the next sweep back. Among the pilots is, I think, left and standing, Le Cheminant; centre sitting, Sexton Gear; and Hardy with his hands on his hips, centre right. The board had hooks on it and the pilot's names were hung on discs on these hooks; all rather primitive but practical.

The Spitfire IX in all its glory. Note the four-bladed propeller and the absence of any bulging air-filter as in the Vs. RN were our squadron letters and we used the same letters on our Thorneycroft lorries. Generally there was a third initial to identify an individual aircraft but presumably this was a new arrival. The picture was taken at Souk el Khemis, about 19 February, 1943.

Roy Hussey in his new Spit IX. See the section in Part 3 on Tom Hughes for Roy's mini biography.

A group of pilots outside the Operations tent at Souk el Khemis. From the left, Sollit, Danny Daniels, Corbin, Smith, Hardy, Paddy Griffin (MO), Scrase and Tom Hughes. In the background sitting is "Cholmondley" Cox.

Some of our pilots landing after a sweep led by W/Cdr "Sheep" Gilroy (fourth from left wearing a battledress top over khaki shorts). Second from the left is Jimmy Corbin, third and at the back is Sgt Pearson; fifth is "Sex" Gear. David Cox is talking to the Wing Commander, while in the right foreground is "Lou" Louis, with tom Hughes next, to the right. "Hoots" Connolly is supporting the Dispersal tent on the extreme right. The five remaining figures cannot be identified. "Sheep" Gilroy, an Auxiliary Air Force Officer, was a farmer in Scotland and a brilliant marksman. He went on to command 324 Wing in Sicily and Italy as far as Naples (November 1943). He died in 1995.

This machine gun was removed by our echelon from a crashed Beaufighter, rigged up by Sgt Wright (who appears on the right), and then sunk into a hole. It was far more comforting to shoot at raiders than just to sit in a trench. Later we also had a pair of Browning guns made up, with which I once claimed a 109 which had been strafing us. It crashed about a mile away but Intelligence refused to credit me with it because it had already been hit by a Bofors Anti-aircraft gun shell from our army guard whose job this really was. We took the Beaufighter gun with us on our Kasserine expedition and mounted it as convoy guard when we stopped.

Richardson and my motorbike talking to an Arab on our way to Constantine for a holiday. This photo was taken somewhere close to Souk Ahras at the western end of the Messerschmidt Alley where the mountains began and the scenery improved. Riding motorcycles about your own airstrips mostly cross-country is one thing; there are always mechanics about who can repair at a moment's notice. But, going a long distance on what you think is your reliable bike is something else. As it is described in the diary, we had a series of mishaps as various parts of the bikes let us down, mostly mine which was a fine old-style BSA with a long stroke but ridden almost to death at Souk el Arba. At this time the pilots were all in transit to Gibraltar via Constantine to pick up their "Spit" IXs. There were only two Spit IX squadrons in the RAF attached to the 1st Army, 72 on our wing and 81 on the other, so it was quite an honour for us. The introduction of the Spit IX in the air battle over Tunisia had a profound effect. One or two American squadrons flying Spitfires were also re-equipped with IXs as a gesture by Churchill to Roosevelt.

Our Spit IXs lining up after landing to have their filters hand-fitted over their air intakes to keep out sand and dust while taxiing to their dispersal points. Correspondingly, after taxiing to take-off, the filter was removed by the ground crew assigned to each airplane at the ed of the runway., During this operation the propellers were kept running and the air intake was comparatively close but we ever had an accident. This simple fool-proof system was the one I ended up with after many experiments with air dropped filters which were difficult to find and got bent in their impact with the ground. The life of a Merlin engine in those days was about 100 flying hours; can you imaging the shortness of this useful life? At 1½ hours per trip this meant only 66 trips so of course, we were for ever changing engines in the Echelon. To make things more complicated, thee were two sorts of propellers, the Rotor and the De Havilland and neither would fit the reduction gear of the other, so F/Sgt Horner had to keep a good stock of both. Many a time we had to change the reduction gear of the engine to fit the only propeller he had available and this meant taking the whole of the front part of the new engine off in appalling dusty conditions. Compare this 100 hours in fighting conditions with today's jets where 5,000 hours life is a conservative figure.

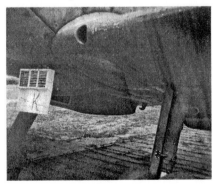

Close-up of a 'Farish filter' on a Spitfire.

Tunis had fallen at last and we were in convoy on our way from Mateur, first to Tunis itself (where we our aircraft participated in a Victory Parade) then down to Sfax where we "shipped" to Malta in preparation for he Sicilian campaign. On the way to Tunis we passed a wreck of an Me109 beside the road. The pilot looking over the wreck is Frampton.

Three smiling members of "B" Flight photographed in front of a Spitfire V, probably at Souk el Khemis.

A telling reminder rigged up by the Military Police, using four-gallon petrol tins. It was one of several warnings posted along "Messerschmidt Alley", a long, straight road running from Ghademou to Souk el Arba and beyond. In the picture F/Sgt Horner (Equipment) is on the right, the driver Cpl Jenkins is in the middle, while the third person is the ubiquitous photographer whose name can now only be recalled as beginning with A ... .

Tom Hughes' forced landing on the other side of the mountains overlooking Souk el Arba. After getting out he checked the throttle control which had let him down and found that it had parted due to the lack of a split pin, proving that there was absolutely nothing that he could have done to maintain power. Then, going by the sun, he headed north back into the mountains since he did not know which side of the lines he was on. LAC Mike McCaul and myself had set out to look for him and we kept going all night. This photo was taken by me next morning when, with the help of some Arabs, we found his aircraft. The full story is recounted in the Diary (Part 3).

The airmen in steel helmets cannot be identified but the hatless driver reclining on the radiator of "Violet", the Squadron 25 cwt, was "Taffy" Coates. Violet was the name of his wife!

My "Oppo" Bill Broughton, Engineer Officer of 243 Squadron; Bill and I found ourselves in parallel with each other for some three years, first at Drem, Scotland, he with 453 and I with 222 and we became firm friends. Then, when 243 came up to join us at Souk el Khemis, Hal Far, Comiso, Pachino, Salerno and Naples, we were on the same 324 Wing. 243 went to Turkey, Corsica and then Dijon on the South of French invasion, before withdrawing to Leghorn before rejoining the Desert Air Force in North East Italy. Shortly afterwards 243 was dissolved and Bill found himself posted back to 113 MU so there we were on the same unit now and at Capodachino again. He went home in October 1945 and I in April 1946. He was a man of 35 to 40, a regular NCO until commissioned during the war. As we were both in effect doing the same job and he had a lot more experience, he was as important an adviser to me as Chiefy Landon, and as good a friend.

A photo of 72's pilots taken in March at Souk el Khemis, with a Spitfire IX and its groundcrew in the background. Back row (l to r): Jupp, Corbin, Gear, Smith, Walker, Cox, Le Cheminant, Oxspring, Daniels, Pearson, Hussey, King, Griffiths, Hughes and Prytherch. Front row: Scrase, Clarkson, Hunter, Sollit, Malan, Hardy, Frampton and Fowler. George Malan is not mentioned elsewhere in the text. The younger brother of the ace "Sailor" Malan, he was brought down and killed by "friendly fire" from the ground in the closing stages of the Tunisian campaign. (Photo donated by L Frampton)

72 Squadron pilots at Arba (left to right) Owen Hardy DFC, Daniel DSO DFC+bar, Tony Fowler, Jimmy Corbin DFC, Le Cheminant DFC, Lewis, Cox DFC+bar

F/O Fergus King joined 72 at Souk el Khemis and won the DFC. He became a personal friend of mine of whom I heard later that he had gone to Kenya, where he died.

Comiso in Sicily was a major German-Italian base for supplying North Africa. We repaired one of these Me109s and made it serviceable for our pilots, especially Tom Hughes who made it his business to translate all the instructions in the cockpit into English. Tom became expert at flying it. It had one peculiarity: one of the undercarriage legs had to be locked down by hand. Tom took care that all the pilots who flew it knew of this odd feature and it was, when we got to Pachino, well used in practice dog fights between a Spit IX and an Me109. The story is told in the diary where Sexton Gear was flying it but forgot to tell the ground defence force in advance so that when he approached to land, they not unnaturally assumed that he was an enemy aircraft. Tom went up to cover him and by weaving his wings gently right and over the top of Sexton, got the Army to stop firing. Unfortunately, the experience of being shot at such close range so distracted Sexton that when eventually he did touch down safely, he forgot to lock the undercarriage leg. It collapsed and the Me had to perform a ground loop which wrecked it beyond all possible repair. In spite of the heavy small-arms fire which had been aimed at Sexton before Tom silenced them, the gunners were mortified that not one shell hole had penetrated the Me109. Nonetheless it was a write off by our own mistake; nor could we find a replacement for it in Pachino. But there we did find something else even more valuable – the "Pisser" as it came to be known.

George Keith's grave near Lentini; Roy Hussey and "Scottie" originally found it from the air. George, a Canadian, was on his first tour of ops with the Squadron and had already shot down eight enemy aircraft so he was looked upon as a coming ace. Then he went strafing near Lentini and unfortunately got hit by ground fire. He managed to fly out over the sea but in trying to bale out at low level, broke both legs. He was rescued from the sea while still alive but died shortly afterwards from exposure. This was in August 1943.

Later while on the road looking for a piano (the story is told in the main text), I made a detour at Mellili to find George's grave which we found after a very winding road down to the sea. The next photo shows a row of four temporary graves with George's being on the left. The other three were all British soldiers. We straightened the cross on George's grave and reinforced the joint. The inscription had been made only in pencil and so we went over it in heavy ink, trusting that it would last until the "follow up" crews from the Army got round to moving the bodies to a war cemetery.

Somebody found this wonderful little airplane in a field near Pachino. It was an Italian Caproni Moth with a six-cylinder, in-line, air-cooled, Alfa Romeo engine. It was in perfect shape and Tom Hughes and I quickly adopted it. I tested the engine as we found it and either Tom or Danny, I think the latter in his capacity as CO, flew it over the tree tops to Pachino. In principal very like a Tiger Moth but slightly larger. How it came to get there was a mystery but the most reasonable explanation was that two Italian Generals borrowed it up north and flew it south to get away from the Germans. It had dual controls for training, would do wizard aerobatics in Tom's hands and flying it on hot southern Sicilian afternoons was a tonic. Tom used to take the ground crews up in it, and me, during which his log book shows 1hr 50mins of instructional training. Without this informal prior experience I could not possibly have dared to fly a Spitfire later on. Tom always said that I tried to land too high, "wait until you can see the tops of the grass waving", was his advice but I never dared and would stall it too high.

The Pisser, as it came to be known, figures in many incidents in the diary so it is redundant to repeat more of its story now. Tom never let me fly it solo correctly. Curiously enough, for all its dual controls the brakes could be only operated from the front cockpit which caused a disastrous mess of the undercarriage one time and required every ingenuity of the Echelon to repair it using Spitfire and home made parts, and it took over a month. When we occasionally moved north, beyond its range, we took the wings off and carried it on our articulated tractor. It even had legitimate purposes such as carrying spare parts for F/Sgt Horner. There was no way we would part with our Pisser.

Jupp takes his turn in the Pisser.

A German transport plane which Roy Hussey claimed he shot up on the ground during a strafing attack from Malta.

A visit to 72 (Basutoland) Squadron at Malta by the "Resident Commissioner" for Basutoland, Lt Col C N Arden Clarke, accompanied by Colonels Syme and Charnock. The Protectorate of Basutoland also sent troops to the Mediterranean theatre; later many were to be lost at sea when their troopship was sunk in the Med.

Back row: Tom Hughes is sitting astride the "prop". Second row (l to r) F/Sgt Hermiston, "Spanner" Farish, Sgt Griffiths, "Sexton" Gear (in topee). Third row: ?P Jupp, Ken Smith, Sgts Connolly and Weller, Eric Shaw (RNZAF), Sgt Scott, W/O Clarkson (RAAF), and Fergus King. F/S Morris is crouching in front of the front row who are: F/L Race (Adjutant second replacement for Tiny Le Petit), Col Syme, S/Ldr "Danny" Daniels (who had replaced Bobby Oxspring as CO), CN Arden Clarke (later, as Sir Charles Arden Clarke, to be the last British Colonial Governor in the Gold Coast), Col Charnock, Roy Hussey, F/O Brill (IO) and Paddy Griffin (MO).

Pilots inspecting a Me109 which had been brought down over Khemis; extreme left is F/O Shaw of New Zealand and on the right is Sgt Pearson. Note the Ace of Spades insignia. In II Group on sweeps over Northern France, the stiffest opposition came from the Ace of Spades Squadron. The Me109 Mk 9 was superior in general to our Spitfire Mk Vs, except in turning, but our Mk IXs were superior to the Me 109 Mk 9s in climbing and diving as well as in their turning circle. It was a technical race between the designers of the Spitfire and those of Messerschmidt, which continued all through the war.

Some of the members of the Senior NCO's Mess, which found a home at the back of M. Columbat's house, where a marquée was erected. The Mess also had use of part of the rear of the house where this snapshot was taken in February/March 1943. Amongst those standing (far left) is F/Sgt Horner, Sgt Sollit, W/O Elton (SWO), Sgt Garland (Cyphers). Sitting on the left of the railings is Sgt Boakes, while F/Sgt Watkins-Field is on the right of those sitting on the steps. It is regretted that other identifications cannot be made these fifty-three years later. (Photo supplied by L Frampton)

Warrant Officer "Chiefy" Norton re-arming a Spitfire with 0.5 Cannon ammunition; his assistant remains unidentified. Norton was both respected and admired by all ranks. The performance of the 72 armourers was second to none in North Africa, as is indeed shown by the statistics in the diary - (Photo donated by L Frampton)

Echelon instrument reps.

The drome in Malta.

Dodge Truck, Malta.

1943 camp stores.

1943 FS Horner in the stores.